MURDER
IN THE
GRAVEYARD

MURDER
IN THE
GRAVEYARD

A FAMILY CULT TRAGEDY

FRANK STANFIELD

WILDBLUE
PRESS

WildBluePress.com

DEDICATED

*To the memory of Sue-Ellen Anselmo,
Jan 1, 1980—March 18, 2019*

FOREWORD

BY FRANK STANFIELD

*"Sure, the movies follow themes that include
politics, murder, high crimes and misdemeanors,
loyalty vs. betrayal, sin (original and otherwise),
revolution, drugs and prostitution, the promise of
ultimate redemption and the obligatory presence
of retribution. But family, that's the key".*[1]

The strangulation of a 39-year-old pregnant woman was
shocking to the first responders who rushed to the scene on
March 13, 2019. But it was the victim's relationship to the
killer, the location, and the unveiling of a family cult that
would fascinate and horrify Central Florida residents for
years to come.

Sue-Ellen Anselmo was attacked by her 20-year-old stepson,
Ian, in a cemetery with its own unfortunate, lurid past.

That cemetery would later serve as her burial plot, more
family violence, and the removal of her body.

---

1. Dan Webster, "Top 15 *Godfather* Quotes About Family, *The
Spokesman-Review*, April 6, 2010.

Allegations would surface about domestic violence, infidelity, mental illness, and lifestyles so dysfunctional Ian's attorney, Richard Hornsby, could only describe it as "crazy." It had been an ugly secret, hushed up by a Mafia-like family code of silence, but it would come to light because there are no secrets in a homicide investigation.

Sue-Ellen was leaving her husband because her adult daughter, Dejah-Thoris Waite, told her that she had been sexually assaulted by her husband, John Anselmo.

Ian's defense would be that he was temporarily insane at the time of the murder. It was "crazy," his attorney would say, but was it legally insane? The jury would have to decide.

I would cover the story from the beginning to the trial for the *Daily Commercial* newspaper in Lake County, just outside of Orlando.

It was one of the most twisted tales I have covered in 50 years, which is saying a lot, since I have written about a teen vampire murder cult, alligator attacks, murdered cops, a teacher who had sex with one of her young male students but was too pretty to go to jail, and too many "Florida man" stories to count.[2]

2. Frank Stanfield, *Vampires, Gators and Wackos, A Florida Newspaperman's Life,* WildBlue Press, 2022.

CHAPTER 1

"I KILLED SOMEONE"

The hair stands up on the back of your neck when you hear Ian screaming, sobbing, and howling like a wounded animal.

"Nine-one-one, recording. Do you need police, fire or ambulance?"[3]

"An ambulance, please!"

The dispatcher could be heard transferring the call from the Lake County Sheriff's Office to Eustis Police. "She's going to be at the Greenwood Cemetery at 220 Hasselton Street. Go ahead."

"Go ahead."

"Yes. I killed someone. She's …."

"Where did this happen at?"

Ian Anselmo: "Oh God!"

Male voice: "Hello?"

---

3. 911 recording, March 13, 2019.

Anselmo: "Please send some help."

"Male voice: "Did this happen at the cemetery?"

"Yes, please."

"Okay. What happened?"

"I killed someone accidentally."

"Can you tell me what happened, please?"

Anselmo: Crying, (indiscernible).

"What is your name?"

"My name is Ian Anselmo."

"Okay. And who is it that you injured?"

"Sue-Ellen Anselmo, my stepmother."

"Okay. Where is she at?"

"She's in the car with me."

"Okay. And what did you do to her?"

"I strangled her (crying). My dad's gonna kill me."

"Okay. Do you have any weapons with you?"

"No, I don't."

"All right. Is she bleeding?"

"Yes."

"Okay. Where is she bleeding from?"

"I don't know. I can't (indiscernible)."

"All right. Do you know how she got injured?"

"I guess I strangled her."

"You guess you strangled her, or you did?"

"It was, I remember we got in an argument (crying)."

"Is she breathing?"

"No, it doesn't look like it."

"Okay. Do you know how to check for a pulse?"

"Yeah. My mom (indiscernible)."

"Can you check to see if she has one?"

"She doesn't (crying). Are the police coming or not?"

"Yes, the police are enroute, sir."

"Thank you."

"What kind of car are you in?"

"A red minivan (crying)."

Male voice: "742. Advised they're in a red minivan. Ian Anselmo."

Anselmo: (Crying). "The police are here"

"Okay. What I need you to do is when you step out of the vehicle, make sure you have your hands up and they can see that."

"Yes sir. Do you want me to (indiscernible) or leave it in the car?" (It is unclear what he is talking about here.)

"You can leave that there. Make sure you keep your hands where they can see them."

Anselmo: (indiscernible).

With guns drawn, officers confronted him and placed him in handcuffs.

Strangely, in body cam videos officers seemed more concerned about him than Sue-Ellen, seen in the background unattended, slumped backward in the front seat, a phone cord wrapped around her neck.

"Are you good? Breathe in," one of the officers told Ian. "We're good? Take it easy, man. Breathe. Don't stop, man." Another officer noticed blood on Anselmo's hands and asked if he was okay.

"I'm fine. I just need some water, anything to drink."

One of the officers, making sure Ian had no weapons, ordered him to quit crying. "Stop, man. Stop it. Stop. Stop, Chill out!"

"In my left pocket you'll find a rosary but that's it." He then added that he had a scapular, "my necklace. You can take everything else off but leave that."

They asked how she got injured.

"I guess I strangled her. I'm so sorry."

Asked if he was hurt, he said, "Physically no, emotionally yes." Then, he said, "I don't think I'm hurt. My name is Ian Magnus Anselmo, DOB is 3/17/1998. My father is going to be so mad."

When an officer called in his name over the radio, he misspelled it and Ian corrected him.

When they asked her name he said, "Sue-Ellen. One word. It's hyphenated."

Ian, who was wearing a dark T-shirt with the image of pro wrestler Bret "Hitman" Hart, was ordered to lie on the grass.[4]

"I'm scared of ants. I have a fear. It's silly."

When an officer asked if he wanted to sit up, he replied: "That's the least of my worries. I'm not trying to be facetious or anything."

When they were taking him to the police station he said, "Please don't forget my rosary on the ground."

That, in fact, would be the least of his worries. Sue-Ellen was alive -- barely. But prayers would not end up saving the 39-year-old or the 6-week-old baby in her womb.[5]

---

4. Trial transcript, Vol. IV, April 9, 2024.

5. Stephen Hudak, "Killing suspect to siblings: 'It could always be worse," *Orlando Sentinel*, March 26, 2019.

CHAPTER 2

"IMMINENT DANGER"

Family members rushed to the hospital. Sue-Ellen's daughter, Dejah-Thoris Waite, went with her grandmother, Cynthia Miller. Sue-Ellen's estranged husband, John, who is Ian's father, arrived with his children. When they saw Dejah, they exploded in savage rage.

John's words heaped pain on top of Dejah's shock. "He said it was my fault his son attempted to murder my mother, and I believe he had a big part in it," Dejah would write in an injunction for protection.

"I am currently caring for four of the minor children to my mom/stepdad and I am afraid he will try to find me. I'm in fear for my safety and there is an ongoing DCF (Department of Children and Families) investigation."

Miller was appointed emergency guardian of Sue-Ellen.

Miller stated in her petition that her daughter had retained a divorce attorney "and recently moved herself and her minor children out of the marital home due to fear for her own safety and the safety of her children."

She moved in with Dejah on March 6.

Miller referred to John as "a person of interest in the investigation." Police soon dropped that idea.

Dejah said John made numerous threatening calls to her mother when she stayed at her home from March 6 to March 13.

She also wrote that she "received texts and calls that I should kill myself."

Dejah said when she lived at the family home from 2014 to 2016, she was "kicked, punched, whipped with a belt and sexually abused" by John.

Injunction forms include a query about firearms, and she wrote that he carried a handgun in a fanny pack and had another seven at his home.

The form also listed his address and the places where she lived, where she worked and the university where she was attending classes.

LOST SPARKLE[6]

On March 18, 2019, five days after the attack, Sue-Ellen's struggle came to an end, sending a wave of shock and sadness across the community.

"She was a wonderful person," said Janice Wilson-Vincent, the owner of the Talk of the Town beauty salon where Sue-Ellen had worked for 14 years.

"Her smile just tells you who she was. She made everyone comfortable and made sure her clients were taken care of.

6. Frank Stanfield, "She started losing some of her sparkle," *Daily Commercial*, March 21, 2019.

When she didn't have a client, she was on the phone making doctors' appointments for the kids."

The children at Dejah's house were 16 months, 3, 4 and 7 years old. One of the youngest was a Down Syndrome child.

Dejah had nothing bad to say about Sue-Ellen. "She was a "great mom."

"She was a very strong and independent woman, super stubborn and extremely caring. She was the breadwinner and paid all the bills. She was very professional and more up to date than most."

Dejah laughed when she recalled her mother telling coworkers: "It's not frosting, it's highlights."

"When she first started working for me, she was a very energetic young lady," Wilson-Vincent said. Toward the end, however, "she started losing some of her sparkle."

Sue-Ellen's coworkers knew Sue-Ellen was leaving John and were nothing but supportive.

No group is more wired to the emotional current of a community than hairdressers, and they rallied around Dejah and her grandmother.

Wilson-Vincent's daughter set up a GoFundMe account to help with expenses.

"They have a long road ahead of them and will need all of the support that we can give. Please be generous in making sure that the thing that mattered to Sue-Ellen the most, her children, are protected and safe," the post stated.

CHAPTER 3

"I JUST LOVED MY WIFE"

John Anselmo fired back at Dejah's accusations in a newspaper interview.

"If there was abuse, why didn't the other kids see it? I just loved my wife."[7]

"I don't want to ruin my wife's reputation, but there are things about my wife that people don't know. We were married 13 ½ years. I'm a stay-at-home dad who is with the children 95 percent of the time. My wife was mentally ill, had bipolar, borderline personality disorder, and adult ADHD."

He said she sometimes tried to commit suicide.

He said Dejah was bipolar, too. He also called her a liar. "She just wants attention. It's pathetic."

"Wow!" Dejah said when she heard his statement.

---

7. Frank Stanfield, "A Family Torn Apart," *Daily Commercial*, March 23, 2019.

"She had ADHD, and she took medicine for that. That's all."
Dejah denied being bipolar or having ADHD herself. "What
do you expect him to say, 'I did it?'"

Sue-Ellen and Dejah went to the Eustis Police Department
on March 5 to complain of John's abuse.

"Sue-Ellen advised that she is fearful of returning to her home
now that she has reported the incidents to law enforcement.
She believes John is possibly 'onto her,' as she is having
difficulty hiding her emotions, knowing the incidents which
had happened to Dejah. Sue-Ellen further advised that John
has seven guns at the home and usually carries one on his
person. She is fearful he may shoot her, himself, or the
children. She stated that he once put his weapon to his own
head and threatened to kill himself if she left."[8]

John told police that she had stabbed him and Ian, had thrown
glassware at the children, and struck him. Police asked why
he never reported the incidents to police. "Because I'm an
idiot and I love my wife."

The report listed the names and ages of the children: Ian, 20,
Eric, 19, Nico, 15, Rajko, 10, Korak, 7, Tars, 4, Grey, 2, and
Moog, 7 months.

"VERY CONTROLLING"

Coworkers said Sue-Ellen did not have friends outside
of coworkers and clients. They described him as "very
controlling." He forced her to wear long dresses, drove her
to work and picked her up. They did not want to be identified
in the newspaper article in which the salon owner said she
had "lost her sparkle."

---

8. Eustis Police Department Report, E19030486, March 5, 2019.

Sue-Ellen relayed her own allegations in the March 5 complaint. She figured Dejah left home in 2016 "to get away from John because he is verbally abusive and very controlling."

In describing how John controlled her, Sue-Ellen, said he monitored her cell phone usage.

"Sue-Ellen has to ask permission to use her iPad or do anything with the kids such as watching a movie or giving them a snack," the report stated.

"Sue-Ellen is not permitted to leave the residence unless John or one of the three oldest kids are with her.

"Sue-Ellen stated that John has hit her in the past and has choked her and the two oldest boys. John has beaten the 15-year-old with a belt. John is verbally abusive to her and the oldest children. Sue-Ellen advised that the children have been 'brainwashed' by John into thinking that Sue-Ellen is the 'bad guy,' going so far as requiring the 19-year-old to watch over her when she is bathing the younger children because he believes she may drown them."

During her separation, Sue-Ellen's father, Jack Miller, took out a trespass order against John at her workplace, complaining that John was stalking her. He also installed surveillance cameras at the beauty shop.

"On March 13, 2019, at 1:44 a.m., the camera recorded a four-second video of an individual walking by the door of the Talk of the Town Hair Design," a defense motion to exclude evidence stated.

"At no time did the person face the camera or show their face or any identifying features," the document stated. The salon is near a motel "that appears to house numerous transient individuals. The identification of Mr. Anselmo is speculative and more prejudicial…."

The video was not viewed by jurors.

DOLAN ATTACKED

Dejah's husband, Dolan Waite, with his sandy-colored hair, aw-shucks smile and muscles hardened by hard work and exercise, could be cast in a movie as a strong, silent type. He is smart, a dedicated husband and father, owner of his own business, and always looking for ways to improve himself.

John told police one of the issues he had with Dejah was that he did not approve of Dolan. It wasn't just verbal disapproval. In 2016, Dolan Waite told Eustis police that John attacked him at Dejah's grandparents' house.

"Sitting on back porch … John Anselmo approached and shoved me over glass tables, continued to threaten and shove me. Scratching and shoving my head against concrete wall. Went on for 15 minutes or so. Finally stopped and left after Dejah-Thoris' grandfather [Jack Miller] arrived."[9]

Dejah secretly took videos of the incident, the details of which were included in the March 2019 police report filed by Dejah and Sue-Ellen.

"The first video starts by John [getting] in Dolan's face and attempting to get him outside. John said he wanted to talk to Dolan away from Dejah and she walked away. You can also hear what appears to be John spitting on Dolan twice…. When the second video starts, John can be seen pushing Dolan several times all the way across the back porch. At one point, John grabs Dolan's face in a violent manner and saying how bad he wanted to hurt him. John said he wanted

---

9. Eustis Police Department report E1p6121170, Dec. 13, 2016.

to take Dolan's eye and that he wanted to break his face. John does tell Dolan how lucky he is that Dejah is there and she won't always be there. During the video you can hear John saying that he does not approve of him dating his daughter because he knows what kind of a guy he is."

Dolan decided not to press charges for what would have been a simple battery misdemeanor.

Dejah wrote a letter to her mother shortly before all hell broke loose to re-establish contact with her, and to explain why she left home three years earlier. John had restricted contact between the two of them. Part of that letter detailed her marriage to Dolan, including their first date.

"We walked around and talked and sat on the bench and looked at the clouds. It was really wonderful, simple but wonderful. He bought me a teddy bear and we drove back to Granny's and my dad pulled in behind us. He banged on Dolan's window and told him to get out, so he did. My dad called me a whore repeatedly and told me to go inside, which of course I wasn't going to. He shoved Dolan's nose and put his key to the back of his neck and said he was going to kill him. Dolan never once fought back physically or verbally and just stayed calm, which upset my dad more 'cause he thought Dolan wasn't scared of him, but Dolan didn't want to disrespect my dad 'cause that was important to him. After the repeated threats he told Dolan to drive away in the car that Ian had been letting the air out of the tires."

Ian's name came up in an earlier confrontation involving John.

SHOT FIRED

On Jan. 6, 2017, a Leesburg police officer received a call about a shot fired in a disturbance at a house. The officer had been to the home 30 minutes earlier and talked to the owner "about a subject making threats to find him and kill him." He said he did not know the man's name.[10]

Two other officers were at the house when the officer arrived. The man said John and Ian, who he described as "Hispanic males," started walking quickly to toward the front door.

A neighbor said the two "charged" toward the door.

The man told officers he grabbed his AR-15 rifle and told the two to leave. He said they continued walking toward the door so he fired a round into the ground near their feet. He said John had his hand in his pocket, "acting as though he had a weapon."

John and Ian walked back to their car, with John yelling that he was calling the police.

The man claimed John told him on the phone earlier that he was going to kill him.

One of the officers said he found a small handgun in the car. John denied having the gun on him when he approached the house. He said his intent was "to kick his ass."

John said he knew where the man was because he gave him his address. He invited him to come, he said, so they could fight.

John told police Sue-Ellen received a phone call from the man earlier in the day asking for a haircut. The problem? He and Sue-Ellen had dated 10 years earlier.

No charges were filed against either man. John complained the "only reason" that the homeowner was not going to jail was "because he was a white male and all of the officers on scene were white."

---

10. Leesburg Police Incident Investigation Report, Jan. 6, 2017.

John and Ian both have a dark complexion. "The family name is "Italian (Lombardy) and Spanish: from the personal name *Anselmo* which is of ancient Germanic origin."[11]

"I made several attempts to explain the facts to John, but he refused to listen," the officer noted in his report. "At that time, I informed John that he and Ian needed to leave the residence."

The March 5 report also touched on encounters John reportedly had with others.

Sue-Ellen said he had been "barred" from a hospital when Tars was born "because he threatened a male nurse."

The report also noted "a review of Eustis Police Department call records shows two prior incidents involving John to include an argument with a trash man over the abusive handling of his trash cans; the other was John's encounter with Dolan."

DAD THREATENS JOHN

John's name came up the year before in a dispute with his 70-year-old father, Victor, but as the victim of aggravated assault with a firearm.

Police in Tavares were called to Victor's home in April of 2016 by John, who said his father pulled a gun on him and threatened to kill him.

"The son said he came over to the house to discuss some ideas for custom knives, which both men create. When confronted by officers, the elder Anselmo admitted he

---

11. Ancestry.com, quoting "Dictionary of American Family Names," 2nd edition, 2022.

pointed a gun at the son after he became upset and started to punch door jambs in the house."[12]

The father said he was afraid his son was going to attack him. The probable cause affidavit said officers could not find any injuries on John's hands.

The elder Anselmo was hit with the weapon possession charge when an officer spotted an AK-47 propped against a wall and a handgun on the bed. The report noted that the senior man had a felony conviction out of California, but it did not give any further information.

The charges were dropped in June. "The defendant is deceased," prosecutors noted in the court file.

FIRED FOR FIERY COMMENTS

John's name came up in 2018 news stories. He appeared before an administrative judge after being fired from Lake County schools as a teacher for alleged "threatening or harassing conduct" on three occasions in 2014.[13]

In one instance, while accompanied by Dejah, he approached a teacher he had worked with "acrimoniously," while shopping. The teacher turned toward her companion to identify him. "Eschewing self-restraint, respondent approached Mrs. ... and demanded to know if she was talking about him. Moments later, while gazing at Mrs. ... breasts, respondent uttered, 'fakey, fakey, fakey.'"

He then said, "that because he was unwilling to fight a woman, he would instead 'beat (her) husband's ass."

---

12. "Man pulls out gun in dispute over knives," *Daily Commercial*, April 6, 2016.
13. 14-003251TTS, Lake County vs. John Anselmo, March 26, 2015, CLAW.US.

He went to the husband's workplace but he was not there.

On another occasion, he had taken Ian and Dejah to the vocational education center to get some documents notarized so they could take college admission tests. The two were homeschooled online. A 21-year-old student in a nearby classroom casually nodded to John.

"Respondent erroneously concluded that Mr. ... had ogled his 15-year-old daughter."

The report said John overlooked the "perceived slight temporarily" and took the children to the parking lot. "At that point, and without provocation," John returned and asked the man if "if he had a "problem."

No problem, he replied. A few moments later the man was joined by his cousin and fellow classmate, and John asked him if he had a problem. When that man did not reply, John said: "Do you little boys want to get your asses beat?"

John's father-in-law, Jack Miller, who witnessed the incident, told John to go home. "After three explicit warnings, respondent returned to the parking lot and drove away." Miller was the assistant director of the school.

Sometime later, Sue-Ellen confronted a school board employee and accused her of trying to "destroy her family" by providing misinformation to the board and called her a "bitch."

The woman, "rattled by the exchange, began to wheel her shopping cart elsewhere." Moments later she encountered John, who exclaimed: "I read your statement and you're a liar."

One or more of the incidents, especially the first two, warranted termination, the report said, but the district issued a written reprimand, and then fired him.

John, seizing on the procedural error of being punished twice, claimed he was entitled to back pay and other compensation. The two sides agreed on a $60,000 settlement.[14]

Less than a year later, John and his family would be in the news again, this time under dramatically different circumstances.

---

14. Bethany Rodgers, "Lake School Board Agrees to $60K Settlement for Teacher Accused of Sexual Harassment," Orlando Sentinel, June 16.

CHAPTER 4

"JAIL'S A WACKY PLACE"

Police were aghast at the sight of bloodied Sue-Ellen with a cord around her neck, and they were baffled by the few facts that were presented to them in the early stages of the investigation, including Ian's."[15]

Guess? Was he on drugs? Drunk? Experiencing some kind of traumatic blackout? Was he insane?

Investigators immediately began putting together a timeline. He said he had lunch around noon, four hours earlier, and had not taken his pills for two or three days.

"States he has had his Vyvanse but not his Lexapro for 2-3 days. Discusses his mental health history and states he has ADHD and anxiety, when asked about depression he says no." Vyvanse is used to treat attention-deficit hyperactivity disorder; Lexapro is prescribed for depression.

"I was supposed to interview him," lead detective Chris Horst later would testify. "When he got back to the police department, he claimed that he was having a panic attack."[16]

---

15. Defendant's statements, 911 call, March 13, 2019.
16. Trial transcript, Vol. IV, April 9, 2024.

Police called EMS and Anselmo was taken to the local hospital. The small department's other detective was already at the hospital with Sue-Ellen, so Horst did not accompany Ian. He went to the hospital later.

The next day, Ian was assigned a public defender at his first appearance. "So, we blew that," Horst said, referring to a chance to question him.

At first appearance, Circuit Judge Brian Welke asked Assistant State Attorney James Argento about Sue-Ellen's condition.

"I don't know," he said. "This is very serious."

"I know it is," the judge replied. He was the one who signed the arrest warrant. He asked what the state recommended for bond. Prosecutors had not set a hard and fast figure, but Argento said he could set a bond for each charge at $50,000.

Welke boosted the normal bond amount for battery on a child from $5,000 to $25,000, and $50,000 for attempted murder instead of $10,000.

When Sue-Ellen died on March 18, the State Attorney's Office decided to wait for the autopsy before upgrading the charges.

Ian called John from jail on March 15 and told him to be sure and drop his upcoming classes at the University of Central Florida. John asked what happened, but Ian said he was not allowed to talk about it. John told Ian he didn't think Ian did it on purpose.

"I didn't. I was confused and scared."[17]

---

17. Frank Stanfield, "Anselmo reveals fears in jailhouse letters, *Daily Commercial*, May 16, 2019.

On the 18th John told Ian over the phone that he wished he had not done it.

"Me too," Ian said.

Ian begged him to get a lawyer and to get him out of jail, but John said it would cost too much – about $75,000.

"That's crazy!" Ian said.

In a handwritten letter to his father, dated March 18, he wrote in all capital letters: I MISS YOU SO BAD! I CAN'T IMAGINE ANYTHING WORSE THAN BEING AWAY FROM YOU! I AM THE SADDEST, LONELIST, AND MOST SCARED I'VE EVER BEEN. PLEASE GET ME OUT OF HERE!!!!"

"The inmate who gives me food is nice, which worries me. First, he asked if I was an 'Ay-rab' (his way of saying Arab), then if I was from Afghanistan, then if I was a Christian. Later, he asked if I was g-a-y, but I said no. Then, he slipped me a note saying he saw what happened on the news, he doesn't judge, he feels bad and could I be his friend? I said 'yes,' then when he left, I told the officer. He took the note. Then, when the inmate left, he came back and tossed me four cookies!"

Ian created a comic book, published in 2017. He told his father to contact the editor, promising that he would write another. "WE NEED MONEY!"

A letter written a short time later was more upbeat, and he tried to ease the minds of his siblings.

The comic book, *Ian Anselmo's Hero Team Collection 1,* was published by Write Stuff Publishing House in 2017. It was the same year that he was listed as the editor of one of his Grandfather Victor Anselmo's books about his career in making knives. That book is entitled *How To Be A Modern*

Day Moro, A Little Book On Street and Knife Fighting And How To Get The Guts To Win.

"Life may be bitter but at least it tastes better than creamed spinach! In other words: It could always be worse. SO LIGHTEN UP YOU MILK DUDS!!!"[18]

In separate comments to his father in the letter, he said he was saying his prayers, asked for prayers and said, "I just want to go home. Really. I miss you so badly, I think I am not-so-slowly dying. This is the longest I have been without hugging you or making you laugh that I can remember."

Seven days later, he seemed to be adjusting to life behind bars. He urged his father to watch cartoons and play with his 10-year-old brother. He said the two of them "can play with all my Paw Patrol toys."

He also urged his father to eat. "Don't worry about me too much. I'll be good. And if something does happen to me, just move on."

However, he said not to worry about that because God's on my side."

A note dated April 2 talked about how he missed his younger brothers and sister. Included was a cartoon strip he drew of "Mr. Mean" and Teddy Ruxpin.

His letter of April 14 was upbeat.

"Let the kids know I WILL be back," he wrote.

"Don't forget to watch my favorite Ninja Turtle for me. And watch it how I would feel…. You'll get more out of it that way."

---

18. Stephen Hudak, "Killing suspect to siblings: 'It could always be worse,' *Orlando Sentinel*, May 26, 2019.

Here was a 21-year-old Mensa-level genius talking about letting his younger siblings play with his toys. It would lead his attorney to call him a "child in a man's body." It was also a picture of an anxiety-ridden adult freaking out – not because he was facing murder charges, or the fact that he had killed his stepmother – but because he was separated from his father and his siblings. Even more stunning was his little philosophical joke in reference to a Scottish psychologist, R.D. Laing.

"Jail's a wacky place. However, I am getting along fine. Does that mean I'm wacky, too? Well, I am in the mental health pod, so probably? But I don't mind. As some dude named Liang once said, 'Insanity: A perfectly rational adjustment to the insane world.'"

CHAPTER 5

FAMILY CODE OF SECRECY

It sounds strange to say it about a young adult, but Dejah, in Ian's defense attorney's words, "ran away from home" at age 18.

Dejah is a pretty, young woman, trim and fit, with long brown hair, and a sweet, ready smile. She is kind, a natural caregiver and a doting mother to her three young daughters she shares with Dolan. She is a smart, hard worker, a nursing student with dreams of becoming a surgeon.

She is self-assured, and why not? She has used her hard life experiences at an early age like a secret weapon in the form of wisdom, not bitterness. That's not to say that she doesn't miss her mother. She sometimes pours out her heart on social media about how she misses her "mommy."

"I left from a sexual assault," she said in her deposition on Aug. 19, 2020. "…and then the night that I left I had also gotten in trouble and had to sleep on the floor and that was just kind of my last straw." The abuse had gone on over a period of a year and a half to two years.

She was determined to go to the home of her grandmother, Cindy Miller. "I had already been thinking about it for a couple of weeks at that point, but I had attempted suicide before and I was getting up to that point again, where I didn't want to be there anymore."

She had also waited until she was 18 so they could not make her return.

In the ensuring two years, she would join the Air Force and get married. John would block communication between Dejah and her mother and her siblings. But she never lost the desire to reconnect with her mother, and it was that yearning that led to her writing the letter that would set the stage for the tragedy that would follow a few weeks later.

"YOU WOULD HAVE FOUND ME DEAD"'

"Dear Mommy: I want to start by saying I hope you choose to read this by yourself and that you decide not to share it. There has been so much I've wanted to tell you and have you there for, but alas, I know even if you wanted to you couldn't.

"I'll start with why I left the house because you never truly got an answer to that question, and at first you blamed yourself, which couldn't be further from the truth.

"To begin, the amount of fights you and my dad had was awful for me. Every time I saw you get hit it was like I was getting hit myself. Every time you cried my heart hurt for you, and it was so terrible hearing you beg for help and for me to be so helpless and not be able to do anything.

"You are not crazy and you don't deserve to be told you are because you get mad or fight back when you are provoked in such terrible ways.

"You may not like my husband, Dolan, even though you have never met him, but he will never lay his hands on me. I have outbursts too when I'm angry or sad and he handles it so lovingly and never raises his voice or hand. He tells me I'm beautiful all day every day and never calls me stupid or any name out of anger. You really would love who he is as a person.

"Watching you and my siblings get hit, and in some cases beat, was a huge toll on me and even myself getting hit was no fun at all.

"If only you knew all the conversations between siblings, because I know far more than both you and my dad will ever know about what they have all thought. Do you really think we are all so suicidal or that there must be a reason we are driven there?

"You're my mother and I never turned my back on you no matter how many times my dad tried to get me to while everyone else tried to rat you about and get brownie points for 'telling on you.' I'd rather get conceded (sic) remarks from my dad than see you get hurt by his words or hands.

"I love you so much and I miss you so much and you deserve so much better. Everything you ever said about brainwashing and just everything was true and I always saw some things but never truly saw the scope of how bad it was until I left. You deserve better and I'm so sorry your life has been what it is."

Parts of the five-page letter are redacted, including two sections of the first page. The entire second page is blacked out, no doubt referring to her allegations of sexual abuse.

"I left so I could have a life and not be stuck in a bubble. I wanted kids, and a family, and to get to have a job, and save money, and buy my own house. Part of me wants to think you are proud of me, but I don't truly know. The biggest reason why I left though was because my dad was sexually abusing me, and it went on for the duration of two years off and on.

"It was so hard on me being pressured in every way to try and replace you because you guys were having issues. I don't fault you at all for any of the issues you guys had, just so you know. I also never cleaned or cooked or did laundry so he could say you didn't do anything and pit us against each other. I did it because you worked all day and were on your feet and deserved to come home to everything done. Dolan does that for me when I have a long day and I do it for him.

NIGHTMARES

"Anyways I wrote a document about some of the abuse I could remember well enough to write for you and I'll paste it here. It's hard for me to read over again or write or think about, and the only person I've ever told in detail was Dolan."

She also wrote: "Do you know how hard it is? I still get nightmares and feelings that I don't like, and it's so terrible no matter how much anyone tries to say it isn't that bad."

After the page-long redaction, she wrote: "So now you know pretty much why I left. I won't say who, in case you show this to my dad 'cause I don't want them to get in trouble, but one of my siblings knew I was leaving and was happy for me. So, when you guys try to say they all hate me and this and that, one of them knew and encouraged me and was happy for me, and I believe one day they too will leave."

Dejah then turned to what would become a haunting foreshadowing reference to Ian. "... Ian had wanted to run away for years and I convinced him to stay, and my biggest regret was not inviting him to come with me. He was my best friend and I can't tell you how often I cry about him and how much I miss him because I shared every emotion with him, and I've been through all of his roller coasters as well."

"I know how sad Nico was when I left, too. I miss her so bad I have a stuffed elephant I keep in my passenger seat just so I can pretend it's her. I can pretend we are rocking out to the pop music we loved so much but couldn't tell anyone. I can pretend I take her to get her nails done 'cause we fantasized it so much. I can pretend to buy her pretty dresses and shoes and get her hair curled and take her places. You know how much I want to just be a normal family so I can be the big sister me and Nico always talked about being. I want to be there for her, I really do, and leaving was so selfish of me, but I just couldn't do it anymore. You would have found me dead.

"And of course I miss all the conversations I used to have with Eric, and I hope he's still pursuing his career in computers 'cause he would do so well.

"Korak and Rajko are really hard for me to talk about, and when I left, I wanted to come back when you talked about Korak and even when y'all just wanted to talk, but if I did, I wouldn't have left again and I knew that's what I needed to do.

"Korak is my baby and always will be, and the day I left I went upstairs and looked at him sleeping in his bed and kissed him and said goodbye. Do you know how hard that is? You must, you're a mom and I'm like his.

"I only have a couple pictures of him, literally a couple, and one is the screensaver on my phone since I've had it. I have it on my wall in my house and a drawn one that Granny got me made on my TV stand.

"He is and always will be my baby and I miss him more than words will ever describe, and the fact that I'm never allowed to see my siblings destroys me. All because I was tired of being sexually assaulted, tired of seeing others hit and yelled at, tired of being trapped in a bubble. I only have a handful of Rajko too, and of course I have his picture on the wall.

"I asked my dad over a year ago for my flash drive with my pictures on it but I was denied. I have 10 years of my life with no pictures…. Ten whole years, not a single picture. Now I film and take pictures all the time, which I know you love to do, but sometimes my dad says it's weird. I must of gotten it from you. Memories mean so much to me.

"I miss Tars of course and feeding him every day 'cause no one else has the patience to sit there with him but you and I.

"And Grey, whom I didn't get to know well, and of course Moog, who I've never even met.

"I'm not heartless and I hope you know that. It's crazy 'cause I think all the time how I think you really feel about this, and then I don't know if you're the same person you were in the all the rides we had together in the car where would just talk. I can't tell if you really want me out of your life or not. Maybe this letter is making it all worse but I hope it brings you peace."

Life at home was anything but peaceful.

"LIKE TRAINING A DOG"

Punishment for rule violations was not just time out.

Some violations were "kid stuff," Dejah explained in an interview on Oct 29. "Other times it was things like not doing well academically. I've gotten in trouble for not making sure my siblings were getting good grades so I had to stay up all night going over their schoolwork with them. I can't remember specifics right now. Honestly, I've blocked a lot of stuff out."

Dejah she explained in her deposition of Aug. 19, 2020. She and her sister Nico were made to sleep on the garage floor without pillows or blankets, were slapped, beaten and berated. The boys had it rougher. They were made to sleep outside, even if it was freezing or raining. From the time she was seven she was awakened and made to do pushups until she collapsed.

Eric, who is a year younger than Ian, would occasionally run away and John would get especially abusive, Dejah said. "...he got beatings to the point where my dad would tell us that we needed to get Eric away from him or he was going to kill him."

Depriving them of food was another form of punishment. She said John would deprive Eric of food for up to 24 to 36 hours.

She described the beatings as, "... kicking when he's down, punching him on his back as hard as he can, anything, slapping to the face, punching to the chest, head-butting, [and] pulling my sister up by her hair, slamming her against the wall."

Eric, in a text to me on Oct. 27, said he recalled a few instances "off the top of my head."

"I remember in school 95s and above were the expected grades for our schoolwork. I remember not understanding a topic in school and not being allowed to sleep until the topic was mastered.

"If I got a bad grade (less than an A) on a final exam, I remember being so afraid to tell him because I was genuinely afraid of the beating that it would cause.

"I was an altar boy and I remember having a hard time remembering the Latin call and responses from the priest, so I had to keep a cheat sheet of what to say and when with me up on the altar, that was always an "embarrassment" to him and would typically lead to sleeping outside, a beating, showing me YouTube compilation of scenes from *The Exorcist* in a dark room, or refusing to let me eat.

"Having pimples was another thing he hated, I still have scars on my back from when he'd aggressively stick safety pins in them to pop them.

"He would actually not let us eat more than a slice of toast to take our medication with and nothing else for days. I remember being so hungry that I'd sneak some food from the pantry when I could; he beat me till I puked it back up

"We would film home movies or play in family bands and if we messed up lines or a note he would smack us, kick us, verbally berate us.

"I remember when we were filming one of the home movies I couldn't remember my line, so he shoved me into a corner and kicked me in the ribs repeatedly. Before I left the house there was still footage of it on one of his cameras."

Hornsby asked Dejah: "When you were in this situation did you realize how abnormal it was?"

"No," she replied. "I didn't know that it was wrong for a man to even hit a woman."

"Until you got out?"

"Until I got out."

She said Ian was beaten "quite hard as well because he's a bigger guy and my dad doesn't like to feel challenged. So, for example, if my dad slapped me in the face and I didn't cry a little bit or wince, he would hit you again because it wasn't hard enough the first time." It was the same with Ian, she said.

"So, it was almost like he was training a dog?"

"Yes."

"I was in charge of everyone else's schoolwork, all my siblings, and if they weren't getting good grades, it was because I wasn't helping them enough."

'FAMILY CODE'

"Did he ever threaten you with what would happen if you did cross him, like your grandfather was mentioning, like the Anselmo Code or something?" Hornsby asked in the deposition.

She said he did, and she furnished copies of text messages to police. "…I sent text messages showing Sicilian loyalty, is what he called it, 'Family Code,' him telling me not to share family secrets. He also asked me to delete all his text messages that he had been sending me."

She said outside the home, "We didn't speak unless spoken to. We didn't talk in public."

"Would he condition you guys? Like, let's say if someone else messed up. Would he be like, 'This is what happens when you, you know when you cross our family, this is what is going to happen to you,' would he say things like that?"

"No one ever crossed a line. He didn't ever have to make an example out of anybody because we never did it. But we also didn't get an opportunity to leave the house to begin with."

Dejah's eyes were opened about the possibility of another life when she attended the local college for two semesters. John drove her to school every day.

"I wasn't allowed to leave that building. I couldn't even go get lunch, go to the library, I had to stay in that building."

Hornsby asked if she was allowed to date anyone.

"No. I asked to go to the library with a boy I liked and I got beaten for that."

When she told another student about her restrictions, he became alarmed. "And he actually stopped me to tell me that with the way I was living in my family and stuff it seemed like I was going to get with an abusive boyfriend or something and he was like, 'I'm afraid for you. You need to call me if something happens.'"

It was the awakening she needed. It wasn't long before she hopped on her skateboard and went to her grandparents' home five minutes away. Because she was rarely out of the house, she had to memorize the route.

"My mother showed up. She was obviously very upset. She was crying. She said that she didn't want me to leave. She was asking about Korak. If you haven't already heard, Korak is basically my baby, so when my parents mentioned him, I would automatically break down."

She described the 7-year-old: "He didn't really know a difference between me and his mom."

John tried to coax her to come back home. He tried but failed to guilt her into coming back to see Korak but he had another pitch.

"He proposed a deal, that if I joined the military, he would let me stay in contact with my siblings, so the following week I signed a six-year contact with the United States Air Force as an air traffic controller. In the weeks after, he took his deal away. He told me I could never have contact with my family."

Losing contact was devastating, she said. "Those kids mean the world to me."

She was discharged a few weeks after entering the service with a medical discharge. John claimed in a phone interview with me that she broke the agreement.

Hornsby asked Dejah to talk about Ian, who she described as her "best friend."

In her victim impact statement, Dejah said: "Ian is only one month and ten days older than me. We thought it was easier to say we were twins. There was no such thing as stepsiblings in our house. We were just brother and sister. The amount of time we spent together was massive. From third grade on, we had the same teachers and spent every moment in class together."

They spent hours upon hours doing skateboard tricks. She said they worked together as a team to take care of their younger siblings.

She said it was their combined imaginations that entertained the kids. They would not only create games for the children but sometimes more sophisticated storylines for their own enjoyment, with silly characters and "alternate dimensions."

They even had a secret language. "We used to call it Spanglatanish. That means, if you didn't know it in Latin, you would say it in Spanish."

"If you had asked me what I had to say about Ian if this had never happened, I would have told you that he was the funniest person I had ever met. His wit and sense of humor was second to none. He would have me laughing until I cried. He would try every day to make me laugh and he would say if I thought it was funny then it had to be, because it was hard to make me laugh."[19]

In her deposition, she said: "The two years before I left, during that time frame Ian ... did not like people. He did not like my mother, he did not like my father, he did not like any of the siblings except for me. Me and him had a very strong relationship. He was going to run away and he was going to write me. I convinced him not to. It was a childish ... he was going to move into the woods, you know, and he was going to find a way to stay in contact with me."

"When I left, my mother said that Ian would make comments about how it was my mom's fault that I had left and it seemed like he missed me and was upset that I had left in the first place and didn't tell him I was leaving."

"For about six months after that I would try to contact my mom only. And my dad, you can read through the text messages and tell who is writing, my dad would text off of her phone. And I can't prove that, but if you read the text, you can tell when it's my mom and when it's my dad writing," she said in her deposition.

"So that became very difficult. I then asked to see my mom. I texted my mom and asked if she would get lunch with me. And my dad texted me on his phone, freaking out. 'Why do you want to talk [to] your mom alone? What do you want to talk about with your mom? Why are you trying to split me and your mom up?

---

19. Dejah-Thoris Waite deposition, Aug. 18, 2020.

"And I said, 'If my mom does not want to see me, then let me know, but otherwise, I want to see my mom.' I never did get to see her. Then for about a year I quit talking to her and I just sent her a text on Mother's Day, I sent her a text on her birthday, and I sent her flowers to her work, and other than that I left her alone."

She quit trying to call, but she did text.

"And you believe that he was probably responding most of the time?" Hornsby asked.

"Yes."

"And you're basically like, 'You can get out,' right?" "I didn't tell her she could get out; I had no intention of her leaving my dad. I never knew she was going to leave him. She thought the reason I left the house was because of her and I never gave her a clear answer why I left. It was my way of giving her peace of mind and letting her know that I agreed with her, that none of this was her fault, and that I still loved her."

To avoid detection, Sue-Ellen called Dolan, who had once texted her. "I don't remember what it was about but he wrote her something nice…."

Dejah, meanwhile, was also being clever. "I changed my phone number many times."

In the following weeks, Sue-Ellen would talk to Dejah on someone else's phone.

"…the first call was to tell me that Korak had got spanked so hard that he had bruises on his butt. Nico was sleeping in the garage and Grey and Moog weren't even allowed outside and basically lived in their highchairs."

Three weeks after receiving the letter Sue-Ellen made a break for it on March 6.

John was to be with Ian at a wrestling match in Orlando.

Hornsby asked Dejah in her deposition why Sue-Ellen wanted to wait until Ian was not home to take the children to her house.

"… she said that Ian had become a lot more aggressive toward her. If Johnny said something bad about my mother Ian would jump right on it and agree to put her down. He had hit her before when I was living there."

What happened next was chaos, confusion, and meltdown.

CHAPTER 6

"ABNORMAL DEPRESSION"

Eric knew something was up on March 6. John was with Ian at a wrestling event in Orlando, and when he went up to Sue-Ellen's room he saw her packing and talking on the phone. She told him she was organizing her clothes and talking to clients, but he wasn't buying it.

Before long, she went downstairs began "checking out the front window." He figured she was "cheating on daddy," something she supposedly admitted doing in the past, he said in his deposition.

"We'd ask her questions. She was very open about some things. With other things she was very flippant and ambiguous."[20]

There was no cheating, according to Dejah. Sue-Ellen ran into an old friend and disclosed that she was being physically abused. "His wife knew about it," she said. The couple invited Sue-Ellen to stay with them. John found out about the conversation because he always checked her phone.[21]

---

20. Eric Anselmo deposition, March 25, 2021.
21. Interview with Dejah, June 6, 2025.

The next thing Eric knew on March 6, Sue-Ellen was opening the door for Dejah, Dolan, and the police.

"And I'm freaking out 'cause I know that I personally don't want her in the home again," he said of Dejah. "And I didn't know what she was going to do because she's lived a much different life than we're used to. She was living a provocative, dangerous life."

"What's provocative?" Hornsby asked.

"Dressing provocatively, posing in provocative pictures."

"How did you see these pictures??"

"I didn't see them."

"So how do you know about them?"

"My father would update us sometimes."[22]

Eric quoted Sue-Ellen as saying: "I'm sorry, I didn't want you to figure out this way, but your father molested Dejah-Thoris."

"And basically, they're helping Sue-Ellen move out, right?" Hornsby asked.

"Yes, and helping kidnap the kids."

"Kidnap the kids?"

"Uh huh."

"And why do you describe it as kidnapping?"

"They didn't want to go."

---

22. She has never appeared in public, or in any photos I have seen remotely dressed "provocatively."

In what would eventually become public knowledge, the children were separated from most of society. The children were rarely away from each other, were forbidden to leave the home, having their own phone, having a driver's license, riding a bicycle, and were prohibited from having friends.

It soon became apparent why Eric used the loaded word" kidnapped."

"She kidnapped the kids," Eric said. "And the really messed up part about this is it happened to me before with my biological [mother]."

"When did it happen to you, how old were you?"

"I was a baby."

"How do you remember that?"

"I don't."

"Okay. So, you only know about that from your father saying that happened?"

"Yes."

The group gathered up the five biological children Sue-Ellen had with John: Moog, Grey, Tars, Korak, and Rajko.

Eric's statements in his deposition revealed his misconception about Dolan (he called him a "drug addict"). Also telling were his comments about "the rules of the house."

"If you're going to date someone, you're going to have to run it through us because, you know, you're family and we want what's best for you. So, she left and she didn't even tell anyone that she had, that she was in love someone or anything like that."

Hornsby asked if anyone in the family was allowed to date.

"We'd never want to. Our mother totally ruined that for us."

"How so?"

"My father was so in love with her. She showed no reciprocation of the love. So, we're always kind of afraid to even get involved in a relationship with someone."

He described Sue-Ellen as "mentally ill" and "volatile" especially during her frequent pregnancies.

"We're not sure what she's going to end up doing to them," he said. "I had to be there with her every time she gave the kids a bath 'cause we were all afraid that she was going to drown the kids."

He also described Dejah as "mentally ill."

"Oh, okay. How do you know she's mentally ill?"

"Oh, because of the way she left, the way she acted when she left, and … we always knew that she had problems."

"But someone would have to tell you she's mentally ill. Who told you she was mentally ill?"

"Oh, we all noticed, but it was my father."

He said his biological mother was also mentally ill.

"Do you know what she suffered from?"

"I don't. I'm sorry."

He said his father suffered from post-traumatic stress disorder.

Eric said he had his own issues, including memory problems.

"So, it sounds like there's a lot of mental illness with a lot of people in the family?"

"Yeah. We all try to be as open about it as possible."

He said the "kidnapping" caused Ian to have "an emotional breakdown with long crying jags. John, for his part, was not eating.

For Ian, he said, it was, "abnormal depression, abnormal depression, heavy depression."

CHAPTER 7

"FREAKING OUT"

Eric's description of Ian was "abnormal depression," but John described it much differently in his deposition.

"Ian was freaking out because he could hear that they had dogs, and I'm always afraid of dogs with my children. Okay. I've had experiences before and I just don't like it. And I'm thinking to myself holy crap, now we have Sue-Ellen, who isn't very good at monitoring the situation, and we have a variable with two giant dogs. So that became an issue. And I have my kids screaming and screaming for me and I am screaming and screaming for them."[23]

This is how Dejah described the dogs in the letter to her mother: "We have two dogs. I found one on the street and took it in. It looked like it had been very abused and we searched for the owners and all. It's a long story, but his name is Buddy and he is very attached to me. He is the sweetest dog in the whole world. We got a dog a couple months ago at the shelter named Ani. She is super sweet, too.

---

23. John Anselmo deposition, March 25, 2021.

"Joseph my cat died. It's a terrible story and I died that day, too. I cry about him a lot and I really wanted to call you and get comforted. I told Granny how that's all I wanted. It was really hard on me the way I found him and everything. But Dolan and I are trying to get this cat at the Orlando shelter that goes up for adoption Monday, a three-month-old kitten, so I hope he gets off of work in time. Puff is still good. She is actually siting next to me while I type this."

On Saturday, Ian, racked with anxiety and having withdrawal from his medications, became physically ill and spiked a fever.

Eric said he looked flushed. "Dark circles around his eyes and he's sitting in the bathtub saying, 'I don't know what to do,' freaking out, 'I feel terrible.'"[24]

John did not take him to the hospital.

"I try to take a lot of … okay. I'm just going to tell you straight up. I do a lot of things myself. If they get busted heads or stuff like that, I just glue them shut. I do a lot of the medical stuff in the house. I always have. We only take them to the doctor when I can't do it, you understand, when it's beyond my control. And what I thought we could do is put him in the bath, cold water, and that worked while I called Sue-Ellen. So that scary, dehydrated, feverish white skin, it was scary. Okay. It went away and he got himself together. He started to shiver, this, that, and the other, but then he just became an emotional wreck."

Eric said they kept him in the tub for about an hour and a half.

After Sue-Ellen moved out on the 6th John began calling, texting, and once showed up at Dejah's home, banging on the

---

24. Eric Anselmo deposition, March 25, 2021.

door and yelling curses at Dolan. The texts would become more layered and more bizarre, stripping bare the behind-the-scenes personality flaws, fears, anger, accusations, panic, cold fury and an eerie foreshadowing of her death.

One reason John called Sue-Ellen was that Ian had not taken his meds for a few days. That set off a flurry of messages accusing her of taking them or hiding them. She promptly made the necessary calls to get the prescriptions filled. His medications would become an issue at trial.

One of the texts mentioned Ian's younger brother and an incident that happened the day Sue-Ellen took the children to Dejah's house.

"Rajko tried to strangle me. You taught him well," Sue-Ellen wrote.[25]

"Rajko is the golden child," Dejah said in her deposition. "In any dynamic he is my dad's favorite other than Ian."

She said Rajko was upset and even tried to slip away unnoticed at one point.

She said her mother was happy to let the children speak to their father. "But when my mom got my dad on the phone and my dad was supposed to say good night to them. My mom said, 'We'll talk about this in the morning. We'll go over everything and you can talk to the kids.' She's like, 'Just say goodnight to them right now so we can go to sleep.'

"And instead, my dad started yelling for Rajko to leave."

Rajko told his father: "The only reason I'm not killing her right now is because there's a baby in her."

---

25. Public records request, 5th Judicial District State Attorney's Office, Jan. 18, 2025.

"And which my dad never told him that was wrong. My dad was just like, 'Rajko, Rajko, you need to leave.'"

Rajko tried to strike Sue-Ellen with a flashlight but Dejah stopped him.

"I left the room because my mom said she was going to try to handle it. They had the door closed. I heard a bunch of commotion. I walked in and Rajko had a blanket wrapped around my mom's neck and was pulling it as hard as he could. And I tried to get him off and my mom's like, 'Don't hurt him, don't hurt him.'

"And I was like, 'Mom, he's choking you. This is not okay.'"

"It was my idea to take Rajko back to my dad because, at this point, he became dangerous," Dejah said.

CHAPTER 8

BEGGING, ACCUSING, RAGE

The texts between Sue-Ellen, John and Ian that fateful week are textbook examples of manipulation, badgering, blackmail, exaggeration, outright lying, and rage -- lots of rage.

The texts, which were released by the State Attorney's Office, sounded normal at first.

"Are you off tomorrow?" John wrote on March 6 at 5:30 p.m.

"Hello? No response."

The next text from him, at 8:21 p.m., was: "You can't steal 10,000 dollars."

"It's not YOUR money," she said in a later text chain, "and I didn't take all of it. I should have after what you've done."

The texts about money, with various figures, go on for days, but the main theme is John begging her to return the children and her disgust and fury over Dejah's accusation.

"Please let me talk to the kids. Please don't try to take my children away from me."

"I don't know who you are anymore," she replied.

Later, he says: "Please let me talk to the boys. You know how much this is hurting them to be away from me. Please talk to me and let me know what's going on. Are you trying to take the kids from me?"

"I have prayed for God to lead me through this process and He has held my hand since I found out what you did. I am continuing to pray and follow his lead."

"I don't know what is going on. Just please don't try to take my children. They are my whole world. Can't we talk? Where do we go from here? I am so confused...."

"You are not confused. You know exactly what's going on."

Eric said in his deposition that his father was despondent.

"He's not even eating, he hasn't eaten anything. I think all he drank was like some Kool-Aid. He's freaking out. He's constantly freaking out. He's constantly calling. He's crying over the phone saying, 'Please let me see the kids. It's my birthday. He tried to see them on his birthday, too (March 10)."

In another text, he tries to convince her that she is crazy. "Please put into perspective that you are with child and off your meds."

"You don't have to be on meds to know that what you did was unthinkable. Nothing to say now?"

In one text he threatens to tell the children personal things. "I still have your notebooks about going crazy and your letters to the kids. Please just talk to me."

He then accused her of cheating on her taxes by claiming "way less" than what she earned.

She doesn't take the bait, however, and talks about prescriptions for the children and doctors' appointments.

He thanked her for bringing Rajko back home.

"You're welcome for Rajko," she texted. "Don't worry about the other kids. They are doing very well and have everything they need."

John also tried to drive a wedge between her and Dejah. "Don't let her destroy your relationship with everyone else. We found her secret diary. She is lying."

He continued his texts with Sue-Ellen, claiming he had stopped her from harming herself and credited himself for exposing her to the "true faith."

John also asked about Ian's missing meds.

"Mine is on the counter," she said. "That should tide him over. I can't fix it until Monday. It has to be called in. He shouldn't be having any problems. Vyvanse doesn't build in your system. I'm not up. I'm in bed."

On Sunday, March 10, she received another text.

"This is Ian: I don't know why you are doing this, and I honestly don't care at this point. All my life I just wanted a mom, and you have denied me that since I was seven. For years I resented you and wanted nothing to do with you. But that is OK. I am able to move past that. Just like that night we found out you cheated on Daddy. I am offering to forgive and forget, the same proposition you always say you regret not taking before.

"Let me reiterate I, who has never done anything to you but try to be loved, will forgive YOU, who has done nothing to show me or my siblings any love. You always said you wanted this opportunity again. Here it is. Just bring back my brothers and come home. Please."

It was followed by another text.

"This is Ian: in our call you just keep saying over and over I have been brainwashed. How is it brainwashed to say you don't care for us when you canceled our family trips over $200 jeans numerous times. Got all the lights, electricity and water and mortgage shut off on us numerous times because you wanted a $300 purse? You REFUSING to rub our backs or get up with us at night while we're sick with food poisoning from food YOU cooked, even though we rubbed your feet daily while you were expecting Rajko?"

He also mentioned Dejah, using her birth name, Chloe. "And Chloe saying Daddy ruined her life is a joke. If it wasn't for him, she wouldn't even be able to read! She only started reading when she was 7!"

When John texted her again, he wrote: "I guess my fears were correct. You stopped loving me a long time ago and just used me for sex. I am so sad!!"

They disagreed on church doctrine regarding divorce versus annulment.

"...I am allowed to divorce, just not allowed to remarry. I'm fine with that. I have no desire to be in a relationship," she said.

John told Hornsby in his deposition that he hoped things would get back to normal. "But I got a lawyer the next day."

On Tuesday, March 12, Ian texted again with more accusations, including stealing the family's mail (she put a temporary hold on delivery).

"Ian, I will call tonight and possibly stop by tomorrow. I did not steal the mail."

"Thank you so much!!!! This is all I want. Thank you thank you thank you!"

John continued his tirade, saying he lost 30 pounds and begged her to "please just see the damn kid! And please give us another chance. I will die without you. I love you so much!!!"

"I will see what I can do about visiting Ian. It won't be tonight, though. I appreciate very much he wanted to share his accomplishment with me" she said, referring to his newly published comic book and a pizza party that John planned to celebrate the event. "Again, I am proud beyond words."

"Are you seeing someone else?"

"No! I've said over and over that is the furthest thing from my mind and I mean it."

On Wednesday morning, March 13, the clock was ticking. At 8:41 a.m., John texted her and said, "Ian is about to walk to your work." She replied that he could not come to the shop. "I have a business to run."

Later, Ian wrote: "There are things I want to tell you and get off my chest, and not in a bad way. There are a lot of exciting things going on for me right now, and I pray you care enough to hear them. Eric and Nico were rude for various reasons, but I have been level-headed this whole time. Please!!!! Don't I mean anything?!!!"

"You are absolutely right," she replied. "You have been. I really am trying to find time. The day is not over."

"Thank you thank you thank you!!! I love you! I just want to speak with you!!!!"

"I love you too."

But there was another text in the state attorney's records, from Sue Ellen to John the day before.

"I can't tell you if you're telling the truth. Ian told me he wants to skin me alive and cut out my intestines and strangle me with them. He said he has no problem telling me he hates me I don't know what to believe."

CHAPTER 9

"A LOT TO DEAL WITH"

"I just couldn't believe it. I couldn't believe what she was doing," John said in his deposition. "And then out of nowhere she calls up and she says, 'Put Ian on the phone.'"

"Okay, okay. I love you," Ian replied. "Okay. Bye-bye. I got to go," he told his father, and he ran out the door barefooted.

"She's going to drive down Washington [Avenue]. Fine. He gives me the phone. He has no phone. He just leaves. He gives me a big hug and that's the last I see of him, okay, until days later when he's in jail," he said.

Hornsby asked if running out of the house without shoes was "abnormal."

"He never left the house before. Okay. You've got to understand this, too. The only time he ever left the house by himself was to play across the street with the neighbor kids. He's now leaving our subdivision and running down the street."

The kids had not been allowed to play with other children for years when they became home-schooled. Dejah and Ian were about 11 years old. It was when John was fired from his teaching job. Ian's attorney, Hornsby, would point out that he installed shutters on the windows, making the house look like some kind of compound. "It's like David Koresh or something crazy."

John said Ian had never left the subdivision like that before. However, in one of the texts to Sue-Ellen, John said Ian was going to walk to the beauty salon. Then, there was the controversial video showing a shadowy figure walking past the salon one night.

"So, he runs down the street. I was trying to get her to come to the house like she dropped off Rajko right there in front of the house. She didn't have to talk to me. The children just wanted to talk to her and see her. They could have just taken their time one by one right there. She didn't want to see anybody. She just wanted to see Ian."

"And finally, she shows up, picks him up, they start talking. The cemetery is right there. Okay. I live pretty close to the cemetery, especially where he got picked up. So really, it's not unusual if they just parked right there in front of the cemetery and they talked. What was kind of weird is that they went inside the cemetery."

They parked near the grave of their parish priest, Father Pinto.

"I had 17 plots. Okay. I had to sell them all. I had Father Pinto's. I had my children's godparents and all my children and my wife."

"The whole thing was weird, man, okay? It made absolutely no sense. So, he was gone for like a half-an-hour, and I'm thinking, 'Oh, crap!'"

John said he began texting. "I thought she had just, remember she had been ignoring all my texts, I thought they had gotten into a fight and she had said something snarky and she had dropped him off someplace. If she had dropped him off someplace, he's not going to know where the hell he is. He's going to be lost. That's what happened with Eric before. Eric has gone on walks and got lost, and then we had to get the cops to try to find him."

John got into the car to look for him, then saw Sue-Ellen's car and a police officer, "and he tells me something bad happened."

He went home, briefed the children, and went to the hospital.

"I stayed with Sue-Ellen the first night. And then they lied about me and they got to where I couldn't be with her and my children couldn't see her. So, for the final days of her life we weren't even allowed to be around her. And then they got guardianship over her without even giving me a summons or anything."

THE WRESTLING BOND

Before he left the house, Ian thought that if he talked to Sue-Ellen everything would be better, John said.

The two had become close when he decided to become a professional wrestler, John said.

"Now, when you say he's a professional wrestler, I mean, was he just going to the training academy to try to become one, he wasn't actually one yet, was he?" Hornsby asked.

"Yeah, he was wrestling. He was actually tag-team champion in the state of Florida. He was in wrestling magazines. Okay. He was a real wrestler. So, he was training. He had been wrestling for six months, really, really wrestling. He won championships, like I said. He was in magazines. My wife loved it. My wife loved professional wrestling," he said.

"I introduced her to professional wrestling when we first got married. I like professional wrestling. And the kids got into it. And we all thought that Chloe was going to be the professional wrestler. But she didn't have the coordination and stuff. And it just turned out that Ian wanted to do it.

"So, I said to Ian, give me an associate's degree and we started training."

That was in 2018, a year before the murder.

"And he was going to school for his other degree, his bachelor's degree. If he would have finished that semester he would have only had two classes and he would have had his bachelor's degree. I mean, he was so close to everything. He was getting a WWE tryout, a for-real WWE tryout. Okay. That's a big deal."

He said, "People were really looking at him. The plan was to get him to Japan."

Ian was to concentrate on wrestling, John said, while he took care of the "cutthroat politics" of the business.

"Okay, so wrestling was something that they started bonding over?" Hornsby asked.

"Big time."

THREAT NOT SERIOUS?

John downplayed the conversation he had with Sue-Ellen about Ian saying he could strangle her with her intestines.

"So, when I hear all this bull crap that Ian threatened her, no. She said Ian threatened her, but that was in the conversation. I mean, I didn't even acknowledge it, and then we started talking about something else and it was never brought up again."

"If she was so afraid of Ian, why was Ian the only person that she would see?"

Not only did John blow off Ian's strangling threat, but also a supposed concern that she had shared with her divorce lawyer.

Dejah was asked in her deposition if her mother told the lawyer she was afraid Ian was going to kill her. "We were worried. I don't know if she ever used the word 'kill' but we were worried that he was going to harm her."

Ian had "become a lot more aggressive," Dejah said. "If Johnny said something bad about my mother Ian would jump right on it and agree or put her down. He had hit her before when I was living there."[26]

"I have read also that she had said she was worried about us saying that she molested Ian the day before this took place to her attorney," John said (if true, he may have read this in an investigative report). "Again, if she's worried that we're going to say she molested Ian, why the hell... is he the only one you want to see with no witnesses?"[27]

John claimed that she cheated on him, at one time took drugs, drank, threw herself down the stairs, jumped out of a moving car, was violent, beat her head against the wall, and cut herself, and slashed him and Ian.

---

26. Dejah deposition, Aug. 19, 2020.
27. John Anselmo deposition, March 26, 2021.

He talked about big mood swings when she was pregnant, going from "very nurturing" to showing signs of being uncaring. "So, all of this later on has been explained to me as postpartum depression and all these other things, but at the time it was just very odd behavior."

He also claimed that she became hypersexual and "raped" him. She became "super religious" when she became pregnant and then stayed that way.

"Okay. I don't want people looking at my wife a certain way and thinking of her a certain way. But I'm in a horrible position, dude. I'm in a real horrible position. I'm trying to save my son at the same time."

He said he was "so conflicted with so many things. My heart is broken that she lied and said I hit her. 1 am broken. But I still love her. And she's still the mother of my children"

Assistant State Attorney Nick Camuccio asked him in his deposition when Sue-Ellen accused him of hitting her.

"I didn't know this until months later. You have to understand, the Eustis Police Department kept me in the dark."

"So, you're saying the first time you realized that Sue-Ellen had alleged that you had battered her or done any sort of domestic violence was after her death?"

"Yeah."

"Okay. When she is texting you about Rajko strangling her, she made references to whether or not that he learned that from you?"

"This is bullshit."

"Okay. Well, that would be another time that she brought this up that was before her death, you would agree with that?"

"I understand what you're trying to do there, but it doesn't work. But yeah."

"Okay. So, these types of allegations that she had made, you were aware of before her death, that's all I'm saying?"

"Okay."

"What she said about my son and what he did to her and trying to say that he learned it from you or whatever is that she said, she told me in a personal text. I only thought that it was Dejah-Thoris who went to the police this whole time until July and said anything. I didn't know that she was saying things about me, too."

"Do you understand?"

"I understand."

"So, when she started saying things, when I read that, I was shocked."

WHAT HAPPENED?

Camuccio asked if he had discussed with Ian what happened in the car.

"I tried to be very point-blank with him as much as possible. And from what I understand, they got in an argument."

"About what?"

"About the children," he said.

"And she said, 'They'll get over it, and that's what set him off., You got to understand, my wife was always saying that stuff. We didn't do a lot of stuff because of my wife's condition."

He described her as "bipolar," and cited her "bad spending problem" as an example.

"… we had two people, and that's something as a prosecutor you can look past, 'cause you want to nail my son to the wall, is there were two people who weren't on their medication in a very messed up situation."

He said it was the first time Ian had been off his meds since the third grade.

Hornsby asked John how Ian was dealing with the tragedy.

"I got to be honest with you, he's different."

"How so?"

He's really sad. He doesn't do it in front of the kids. He waits 'till later on, and we can have our alone time, talk like adults."

"Right. And what do you guys… what's going on?"

"He killed his mother, man. That's a lot to deal with."

John Anselmo deposition, March 26, 2021.

Dejah deposition, Aug. 19, 2020.

CHAPTER 10

NO REST, NO PEACE

There was no rest in peace or any other kind at the Greenwood Cemetery six weeks after Sue-Ellen's death.

Saturday, April 20, started out with what Dejah thought would be a nice tribute, but things soon spiraled out of control.

Someone had been removing flowers from her mother's grave, and she complained about it to cemetery staff and police.

She was taking flowers to the grave three times a week.

"They were gone. Anybody who brought flowers, they were gone. My mother-in-law would drive around the cemetery looking for them. It turned out they were being taken to other graves and we would bring them back. That went on for a little while," she said in her deposition.[28]

Cemetery workers suggested Dejah hide a trail camera to catch the culprits. Sure enough, John and two children could

---

28. Dejah-Thoris Waite deposition, Aug. 19, 2020.

be seen removing flowers and one of the kids wiping out a love message in dirt with his shoe.

Police said John had the right to remove the flowers since he purchased the plot.

To compensate for what she called "a jerk move," Dejah invited Sue-Ellen's friends to bring flowers.[29]

"… the day before Easter, Easter was the first holiday I had with my mother gone, I wrote a post on Facebook asking any of her friends if they would like to come and bring flowers to her grave; I was going to be there all day. They couldn't be removed because I had a restraining order against my dad so he couldn't be there," she said referring to the injunction for protection she took out when her mother was in the hospital.

About 100 people showed up. "I got the chance to meet some of the people who had been bringing flowers," Waite said. "It was nice."

"I decorated the grave real pretty so that on Easter morning I had some sort of … closure."

The peace was shattered just before 2 p.m. Dejah and a friend had gone to her grandmother's home to use the bathroom. They had just returned when Dejah's mother-in-law, Sharon Sebree d saw John's van suddenly stop, Nico jumped out screaming at Dejah.

"You killed my mother!" She ran up to Dejah and began kicking her, grabbed her by the hair and pulled her to the ground while shouting, "I'm going to kill you!"

Sebree tried to pull her off.

---

29. Frank Stanfield, "A family at war," Daily Commercial, May 6, 2019.

"She cursed at me and then punched my arm and kicked me repeatedly," Sebree said.

Rajko jumped out of the van and joined the fray.

"She immediately turned to me and tried to choke me and started grabbing my hair, pulling me to the ground. At this point I don't want to hurt her. She's my sister. She's who I told I was leaving the house. Me and her had a very close relationship. And she's like, 'You killed Mommy!'

"And I'm like, 'Nico I didn't kill your mother.'"

"You took her off life support!"

"I'm like, 'I didn't take her off of life support.' So, then I see Johnny standing over there in the distance, and I'm like, 'So this is what you are telling them? I killed her? You're telling them I took her off life support?'"

She didn't have the authority to do it even if she wanted to.

"And so, I'm talking to her. Every now and then I say something where she like loosens her grip and looks at me, and she's like, 'No, you're lying.'"

. Dejah would later say that Nico had been "brainwashed."

"So, I continue to just get beaten up by her because I don't want to hurt her. Everyone else is trying to help. I'm telling them, 'Better not hurt her. She has little fingers. Don't break them.'"

"I told [Rajko] to go back to the van," Sebree said. He had kicked and scratched Sebree but he eventually went back to his father. Meanwhile, the group of visitors held Nico down.

"I held her head so she would not try to bite Chloe's arm," friend Nancy Carrier Semento said, using Dejah's birth name in her statement to police. "The young kids acted crazy."

"We could have used brute force to remove [her] hands, but it would have caused injury to [her]," Sebree told the *Daily Commercial*. "None of us wanted that. We didn't fight back, but simply tried to keep her from biting Dejah, or worse, until police got there."

"The police get called, my uncle calls the police. The police show up. They have to fight to get Nico off of me," Dejah said.

"I told them that they can't monopolize the grave," Nico told police. "Out of frustration for their rudeness, I kicked the flowers over."[30]

She was charged with two counts of misdemeanor battery as a juvenile.

John would not comment, except to say, "I think what they're doing is disrespectful to our faith." He declined to elaborate.

Dejah said she had two goals: "I want my siblings to get counseling and I want custody. I still love my sister. I just want him to stop telling lies to her."

If taking flowers from the grave was a "jerk move," what came next was a shock: John ordered Sue-Ellen's remains to be disinterred and cremated.

"I'm extremely upset that we can't even put flowers on the grave, or that he didn't notify anyone about moving her," Dejah said. "I'm just hurt that he's going to this length to spite me. He should let us grieve in our own way."

John refused to comment when contacted by the *Daily Commercial*. He did, however, send a 1,500-word statement to the *Orlando Sentinel* complaining about Dejah and her in-laws. He said they made the site "look like a yard sale as

---

30. Eustis Police Department report E19041897, April 20, 2019.

they danced, trampled and chatted on her grave like pagans while camping out with lawn chairs all day." He said: "It is a sacred place of prayer for the dead's soul."

"I am devastated and beyond hurt that he destroyed her beautiful body in that way," Dejah said. "I broke down when I found (out) …."

She described the family as "traditional Roman Catholics," and said Anselmo told the family that cremation is a sin.

"My mother would have never wanted that. "It is a sin, but it was not her decision, so God has taken her into His arms. He thinks he destroyed her body, but she is in heaven raising her baby girl, and that keeps me smiling."

CHAPTER 11

"WE PRAY WITH HER EVERY DAY"

What role did religion play in the Anselmo family's lives?

"I'm traditional Roman Catholic," John said, not referring to mainstream Catholicism. He is a Sedevacantist.[31]

"We don't follow the Second Vatican Council," he said.

The Second Council, dating from the early 1960s, was sparked by Pope John XXIII "to bring the church up to date."[32]

Suddenly, Mass could be done in another language besides Latin, and priests could face the congregation so they could be heard.

"...the church "officially abandoned its 'one true church' position and formally ended the thousand-year schism with the Greek Orthodox Church. It also entered ecumenical conversations with other churches with the hope of establishing greater Christian unity."

31. John Anselmo, deposition, March 25, 2021.
32. Britannica.com/topic/Roman_Catholicism, Feb. 25-225.

It also recognized the legitimacy of Judaism and condemned anti-Semitism. Pope John Paul II, who was later declared a saint, prayed with world leaders, made a pilgrimage to Jerusalem and prayed in a mosque and a synagogue.

"We have a trinity and Latin Mass, and there's a lot of things of that nature that are completely different," John said. So, we don't follow the pope and we don't follow the new stands that they put in place. So, we're old school."

Church websites refer to the movement as a "schism," even heresy.[33]

Whether the changes are good or bad is up to Catholics to decide. But what it did was to further isolate the family. As few as 20 people attended services, and seniors were dying off, John said.

John claimed Sue-Ellen lost half her clientele when she became a Catholic. "...most of her clientele was part of her church," he said, referring to a Baptist church in town, "and they just dropped her, man."

"We were very close with our priest," John said of Father Pinto. "And he was Ian's best friend. And Ian was going to be a priest."

Ian and Eric were altar boys. He later decided he wanted to be a pro wrestler, illustrator and writer.

The priest died during the time of the alleged affair, according to John. "It was just a horrible year." Anselmo, of course, was referring to Sue-Ellen allegedly cheating on him years earlier, which Dejah insists never happened,

---

33. Fr. Richard Hellman, "What approach should we take with Sedevacantists? Stay Clear and Pray for Them," Roman Catholic Man, Oct. 21, 2020.

The priest's burial spot was next to the Anselmo family plots.

"After all the crap that they pulled with my wife, I had to get special permission and everything to have her exhumed."

He erected a columbarium. "You house an urn. It's in my home. And I have Catholic relics and stuff like that from Padre Pio, her favorite saint. Whatever, doesn't matter to you," he told Hornsby during his deposition.

"But she is more part of our family now than she ever was before. She's part of everything, movie time, games, this, that, and the other. My wife is always there. We pray with her every day."

So, what are the rules for Catholic burial? Dejah said John told her that cremation is a sin. It appears that changed, however, in 1963 during the Second Vatican Council, which he otherwise rejects.

Hornsby, in Dejah's deposition, asked about the current Vatican Council.

"I have no idea. I don't follow up with that anymore."[34]

"But he used to preach that pretty hard to you?"

"Yes. What I realized the Catholicism that we followed really meant and what he did are a little different. His theories are a lot more cultish …."

"Cremated remains are considered the same as intact bodies – cremation was first permitted by the Vatican in 1963 and part of canon (church) law since 1983. But urns are to be placed in mausoleums or columbariums, not kept at home, and cremains are not to be scattered or split up," according to Father Patrick Carrion, a priest for 40 years and the

34. Dejah-Thoris Waite deposition, 2020.

director of the Office of Cemeteries for the Archdiocese of Baltimore.[35]

"It's a lot for this kid to deal with sometimes that he has…. I mean, it's like, it's really heavy," John said. It's really messed up that I have to have her in my home and not buried in the ground like she was before because of what they were doing. Everything is messed up. But he's dealing with it the best that he can but he's very sad, very sad."

---

35. Kurt Jensen, "What's allowed – and not – in Catholic burial and burial practices," *Catholic Review*, Nov. 2, 2023.

CHAPTER 12

INSANITY DEFENSE

On Sept. 20, 2020, Hornsby showed his cards with the following court motion: "The defense intends to show that on March 13, 2019, Mr. Anselmo did suffer from a mental illness, infirmity, or defect, to wit: Insanity and because of such condition, Mr. Anselmo could not appreciate the wrongfulness of his actions at the time of the alleged offense and did not know what he was doing or, if he knew what he was doing, did not know what he was doing was wrong."[36]

It wasn't a big surprise to Camuccio. "It was either going to be a plea with some kind of mitigation like self-defense or insanity," he said.[37]

An insanity plea is no gimme. The law presumes people are sane, so defense attorneys have the burden of convincing jurors that their clients are insane "by clear and convincing evidence." It is the state, not the defense, that usually has all of the burden of proof. They still have to prove the murder charge beyond a reasonable doubt, which is a higher bar.

---

36. Amended notice of intent to reply on the defense of insanity, May 26, 2023.
37. Frank Stanfield, interview with Camuccio, March 10, 2025.

The law was changed following John Hinckley's attempted assassination of President Ronald Reagan in 1982. He was declared not guilty by reason of insanity when a federal judge placed the burden of proof on the prosecution to prove that Hinckley was not insane. Members of Congress were incensed, so they passed the Insanity Defense Reform Act of 1984.

"… the insanity defense is used in only 1 percent of all criminal proceedings, and its success rate is only 25 percent of that 1 percent. Therefore, less than 1-in-400 defendants are found not guilty by reason of insanity in this country."[38]

Hornsby may be a little hyper sometimes, but he is no fool. The board-certified attorney doesn't stroll into a courtroom so much as he appears to rush for an opening like he did when he played football for the University of Florida in the 1990s. He earned his law degree at UF, a master's degree in criminal justice from the University of Central Florida and a master's in pharmacy and pharmaceutical sciences at UF.

He's also media savvy, offering himself up as a law expert sometimes for TV and the *Orlando Sentinel*.

Camuccio is even keeled and quick with a joke, but he has a streak of bulldog in his personality, sinking his teeth into sketchy testimony and latching on to evidence to the end. He played rugby in Gainesville and Orlando. He graduated from UF in 2000 and worked briefly for a small firm until going to work in the State Attorney's Office. He is the go-to homicide prosecutor in Lake County. He was joined in the case by Assistant State Attorney Tom Wiezorek.

---

38. Susan J. Lewis, "Not Guilty By Reason of Insanity," *Psychology Today*, Feb. 6, 2020.

"The prosecutor is not being very flexible," Hornsby said of trying to reach a plea deal.[39]

That was no surprise either. After all, Ian confessed in his 911 call. But then there was this: "I guess I strangled her. I don't remember doing it. I remember the argument."[40]

When officers arrived, they asked if he was hurt. "Physically no, emotionally yes."

He also talked about being without his medications.

One of the biggest problems is that jurors have a hard time accepting the concept that someone can become insane briefly. The reaction of people reading news accounts of vicious crimes often say, "that person must be crazy," but it's not the legal definition.

It is easier to prove if the person has a history of psychological problems like schizophrenia, according to John Spivey, a longtime former public defender who was not associated with the case.

Another hurdle is overcoming the idea of someone who suddenly "snaps."

"Unrestrained passion or ungovernable temper is not insanity, even though the normal judgement of the person is overcome by passion or temper," the jury instructions read.

SHOCKING CASES

Testimony in such cases can be shocking, even to veteran reporters.

---

39. Frank Stanfield, "Anselmo double murder trial pins experts against each other with insanity plea," *Daily Commercial*, June 8, 2023.
40. State's discovery exhibit, April 24, 2019.

Virgil Hyde III was arrested in 2016 for killing his long-time girlfriend and mother of his two young children, Bobbi Wheeler, after shooting her 24 times while she was doing laundry. He claimed that he shot her in self-defense. "She was poisoning me with my drinks and my cigarettes."[41]

He claimed someone sprayed his cigarettes with formaldehyde when he was sleeping, and that someone was hiding in the attic. Jurors watched hours of eerie nighttime surveillance videos where he whispers to Bobbi about what he thinks are neighbors flying drones and sneaking around outbuildings at the couple's rural Groveland home.

What set him off, lawyers said, was a dispute with a neighbor about the legality of having a mobile home on the property.

He even had a rare condition known as Capgras Delusion, the belief that imposters had taken over the appearance of his two children, a defense expert concluded. He was also diagnosed with episodic schizophrenia, extreme paranoia and psychotic delusions.

He thought his parents were working against him when he tried to wheedle more money out of them. His mother purchased their 50-acre spread for $675,000 in cash. At one point, he sent a picture of himself holding a gun to his head.

Prosecutors argued that what led to the tragedy was Wheeler threatening to leave him if he didn't stop using drugs. She was also furious when she learned he had $150,000 stashed away in the bank when he had been badgering her mother for money to pay the light bill.

The state's expert disagreed with the idea that Hyde didn't know what he was doing was wrong. The lead Lake County sheriff's detective testified that it was not unusual for

41. Frank Stanfield, "Defense: Hyde 'Insane' when he killed girlfriend, *Daily Commercial*, Oct. 5, 2018.

defendants to be paranoid. And Assistant State Attorney Jonathan Olson presented evidence that Hyde's behavior could be explained with drug use. He wasn't just taking oxycodone pills, he was crushing them and snorting them, he said.

Hyde's own words helped convict him of second-degree murder. "I lost my cool," he told detectives.[42]

His mother wept when she heard the verdict. "No one wants to believe there's something wrong with their child."[43]

Then, there was the case of Jeremy Main who drowned his 7-month-old daughter in 2017 when his wife said she wanted a divorce. He had a horrible childhood, witnesses said, and a psychologist said he suffered borderline personality and schizotypal disorders. The prosecutor asked her what Main was thinking.

She didn't ask, she said. "It was not necessary. The risk factors were in place."

The jury, however, concluded that it was a case of revenge, not insanity when they learned he called his wife and told her, "You're going to have a bad day."[44]

In 1980 a woman was found not guilty by reason of insanity when she drowned her 4-year-old twin girls and her 2-year-old daughter while bathing them.

Diane Evers said she had her first hallucinations during childbirth in 1977. In one of them, a nurse congratulated her

42. Frank Stanfield, "Hyde guilty of murder," *Daily Commercial*, Oct. 9, 2018.

43. Frank Stanfield, "Justice delayed," *Daily Commercial*, Dec. 13, 2018.

44. Frank Stanfield, "You're going to have a bad day," *Daily Commercial*, Feb. 26, 2019.

for giving birth to twins. "And I said, 'What? I just had one baby,' and then she said, 'Oh my God, you didn't know?' Three doctors told her, 'Mary, we've got to give you a shot of LSD to see if you're the true mother of Christ.'"[45]

At one point, she said she heard a voice coming out of a cloud saying, "Mary, mother of Christ, is that you in a halter top?"

She would spend decades in mental hospitals, diagnosed with borderline personality and schizoaffective disorders. Sometimes staffers would say she could be released but she would "decompensate." During one such an episode she tried to saw her arm off.

In 2013, the court ruled that she could be moved to a lower-level treatment facility.

EARLIER VICTORY FOR CAMUCCIO

Ironically, one of the people who befriended Ian in jail was Ryan Thornhill.

Thornhill walked into a barbershop in Mount Dora in 2017 and demanded that he get a haircut for $2 instead of $10. The barber gently escorted him out and told him to come back when he had $10. He came back a few minutes later with a gun he had stolen from his father and killed the barber.

His lawyer claimed he was insane. Thornhill, who has attention deficit disorder, weaned himself off Xanax and a doctor discontinued an anti-psychotic drug and prescribed a stimulant for ADD. Defense experts said he was bipolar and had had schizoaffective disorder with "breaks in reality."

---

45. Frank Stanfield, *Vampires, Gators and Wackos, A Florida Newspaperman's Life*, WildBlue Press, 2022.

The trial was delayed when lawyers had a hard time finding jurors whose family had not been touched by mental illness somehow or were themselves affected.

Thornhill, who had a history of drug abuse, was found guilty of first-degree murder when witnesses said they smelled alcohol on his breath.

Jurors might have been swayed if a key witness had not backed out of testifying at his trial. His sister, in her deposition, said that he told her he was going to hell to take care of someone who had hurt her as a child, that he needed "more power" to finish what he was he was doing, and that he could see into the future so he put a circle of protection around her so all the darkness would come to him.[46]

Camuccio was the prosecutor in the case. "There were a lot of similar types of issues," he said.

---

46. Frank Stanfield, "Jurors in Ryan Thornhill trial hear defense's arguments for insanity," *Daily Commercial*.

CHAPTER 13

UNDERSTANDING "CRAZY TALK"

Weeks turned into months, and months into years as the case dragged on through the court system. There were the usual motions for continuation begging for more time to prepare, judges retiring and other issues, but the biggest hurdle was Covid in 2020.

Lawyers did what they could, filing motions, taking depositions via Zoom, and working on plea deals, especially for misdemeanors. Public Defender Mike Graves called it dealing with "low-hanging fruit." The emphasis was trying to avoid crowding people together in big groups, like a jury selection for a first-degree murder trial.

In March 2024, Camuccio filed a motion to limit defense evidence.

"Based on the review of depositions, interviews, reports and other documents, the state anticipates the defendant will seek to introduce evidence of the following concerning the victim:

- Mental health diagnosis of the victim Sue-Ellen Anselmo.

- Potential medications for the treatment of those mental health issues of the victim….

- Prior illicit drug abuse on the part of the victim ….

- Prior suicide attempts on the part of the victim Sue-Ellen Anselmo."[47]

He quoted a Florida statute: "relevant evidence is evidence which tends to prove or disprove a material fact." He then referenced another law: evidence that misleads or confuses a jury that is "more prejudicial than probative is inadmissible."

He concluded by saying "The prior issues of the victim are not pertinent to either the elements of the charges, or the defense of insanity."

One of the favorite ploys of defense attorneys is to try to get jurors to look at anyone other than their client. Camuccio's goal was to keep the focus on Ian.

There was another unspoken truth: Sue-Ellen was not alive to defend herself.

Hornsby had to have that in the back of his mind. How would it look to jurors if he assaulted her character? John, in his staunch defense of his son, was putting the blame on Sue-Ellen.

Circuit Judge Brian Welke would later weigh the argument just before John testified at trial. "John Anselmo is not on trial. Sue-Ellen Anselmo is not on trial."[48]

But Hornsby argued that the case was all about Ian's mental state. He said he had to let John Anselmo testify about Sue-

---

47. Nicholas S. Camuccio, Motion for Order in Limine, March 12, 2024.

48. Frank Stanfield, "Anselmo murder trial: Victim's husband and three of her children testify," April 11, 2024, *Daily Commercial*.

Ellen's mental health, if it was true or not, if the jury was going to understand all the "crazy talk."

"...I understand that it's not about John Anselmo, but it's about what John Anselmo told this kid over the years and in the days leading up to this."

It was critically important to know what Ian was thinking when the children were removed from the home, how he reacted when he was off his medication, and how it led to a psychotic break when the two argued, Hornsby said.

Camuccio argued that a past suicide attempt by Sue-Ellen was not relevant.

"I get it, Judge," Hornsby said. "What you're saying about this isn't about John Anselmo. What information he fed Ian Anselmo. If we just say Ian was scared for his siblings, that doesn't make sense. Why would he be scared for his siblings? But if they understood the craziness with which he was fed information, then it suddenly makes sense."

CHAPTER 14

BRAINWASHING VOODOO?

Famed defense lawyer Clarence Darrow once wrote: "Choosing jurors is always a delicate task. The more a lawyer knows of life, human nature, psychology, and the reactions of the human emotions, the better he is equipped for the subtle selection of his so-called 'twelve men, good and true.'

"In this undertaking, everything pertaining to the prospective juror needs to be questioned and weighed: his nationality, his business, religion, politics, social standing, family ties, friends, habits of life and thought; the books and newspapers he likes and reads, and many more matters that combine to make a man; all of these qualities and experiences have left their effect on ideas, beliefs and fancies that inhabit his mind.

"Understanding of all this cannot be obtained too bluntly. It usually requires finesse, subtlety and guesswork. Involved in it all is the juror's method of speech, the kind of clothes he wears, the style of haircut, and, above all, his business associates, residence and origin."[49]

---

49. *"How to Pick a Jury,"* Clarence Darrow, Esquire magazine, May 1936

The phrase "cannot obtained too bluntly" refers to the process of *voir dire*, which translated means "to speak the truth."

The reason jury selection is important is because it is everything that matters: a guilty verdict, acquittal or hung jury. Nothing else comes close, not the evidence, the lawyering, the setting, or even the truth of the matter.

I once heard a lawyer ask prospective jurors what bumper stickers they had on their cars. If the case garners a lot of media attention, like the vampire case, it might be important to find out how they get their news, and what they think about the coverage.

More than a few knew something about the vampire case because it was so widely publicized, but that was not the issue legally. Could they set aside what they had learned, listen to the evidence that would be presented in court, and render a fair and impartial verdict?

Every case is different of course. In the 1990s, Bill Gross, the lead homicide prosecutor for Lake County routinely asked for a show of hands of anyone whose family had been touched by murder. Inevitably, one or two people out of 50 would raise their hands. Now, the number would surely be higher.

He also asked veterans if they had seen combat, presumably to see if they could handle seeing autopsy pictures or listen to one more example of inhumanity to man.

The attorneys in the Anselmo case began the process of selecting a six-member jury with two alternates from a pool of 60 on April 8, 2024.

When it was Hornsby's turn to ask the questions, he led off with the understatement of the year, "…this case is a little bit different than your typical criminal case because the issue of insanity will be raised."

But that would come later.

There were the usual questions about their experience with law enforcement, whether a police officer is more credible than others, and other queries to check for fairness and objectivity.

They were also asked to introduce themselves and tell something about how long they have lived in Lake County, where they moved from, their educational background, their occupation, age, marital status and where they worked, children, hobbies, and if anyone in the family was an attorney or in law enforcement. Yet another question was whether they had ever served on a jury.

Among the uncomfortable questions was whether they had ever been arrested or been involved in a lawsuit, or any of their family members.

They were also asked if they knew any of the parties, including witnesses, or what they knew about the case.

One person said he had read one of my stories in the *Daily Commercial* about how the trial would be about an insanity defense.

"Based on what you saw, you have no preconceived notions about guilt, innocence ..." Camuccio asked?

"No."

Judge Welke then read the legal definition of insanity and asked the following question: "Are you or an immediate family member or close family friend employed in, or have formal training in any field involving psychology, psychiatry, pharmacology, counseling or mental health?"

At least one person raised their hand. It involved a family member who was doing research on Alzheimer's Disease

The judge then asked: "Have you, an immediate family member or close family friend ever been diagnosed with a mental illness such as depression, bipolar disorder or schizophrenia?"

A handful raised their hand regarding family members. The judge said people could discuss the issue at the bench with the lawyers and himself, or from their seat, their choice.

He then asked, "Have you, an immediate family member or close family friend ever been subject to Baker Act proceedings or been committed for a mental illness?"

The last question asked was whether anyone had been the victim of domestic violence, and two women raised their hands.

After the lunch break there were the usual concerns about how long the trial was expected to last (five days), concerns about work, and concerns about "judging others," but some said they were interested in serving. One man seemed to be saying he was having trouble with the nature of the case itself. "I'm about to crawl out of my skin."

One woman said she was, "just angry about the crime against a pregnant woman. I'm angry at that."

Camuccio said that was a normal reaction, the point is, everyone is entitled to a fair trial, including the notion that the defendant is innocent until proven innocent. Could they listen to testimony and compare it to the evidence? Could they discern intent? What about circumstantial versus hard scientific evidence?

The prosecutor went back to those who raised their hands on the various issues, including mental health. One man said he had a 15-year-old son that was being treated for mental illness. He said he could be objective. One woman said her sister died and there were suspicions that domestic violence was the cause. She, too, said she could be objective.

During an afternoon break, however, the lawyers and judge agreed that 12 should be "struck for cause" for various reasons, including one juror who wanted to talk in private about mental health issues.

When it was Hornsby's turn to ask questions, he said he wanted to know about their experiences. "Obviously, you know, we don't want you to be your own expert or to supersede ... the evidence you hear on the stand."

He said he would ask questions about their "belief system" about mental illness.

"Also, gonna ask you a lot of questions about family dynamics. Things like homeschooling versus public schooling, or schooling in general. Not necessarily public, it could be public, private, whatever. Ask you questions about, you know, orthodox beliefs, or extreme or conservative beliefs."

He spent a great deal of time engaging the group, getting them to share their perception of the law. Then, he asked, "Is there anybody that has a belief that mental illness is over diagnosed or used as a crutch currently in society?"

Some said yes. He also asked if it was under diagnosed.

As for insanity, one juror said, "I definitely think that mental illness is and should be factored in ... but I don't think it would erase what they've done."

Hornsby noted that mental illness, like bipolar disorder, is not a defense for a particular crime. The only recognized mental health defense is insanity, and he noted that there was a difference in what a doctor might say versus the legal definition.

"... the Legislature hasn't made it necessarily easy," he explained. There must be proof that he did not know what he was doing was wrong.

One question was directed at a person who had homeschooled their children.

Hornsby wondered how they would react to dueling psychological experts.

"... the scenario I'm giving you though is, let's say you find my expert credible. You find the state's expert credible, but you find that my expert was clear – and clearly and convincingly proved – convinced you that he was insane at the time of the offense right, will you be able to return a verdict of not guilty by reason of insanity even though you at the same time found the state's expert credible?"[50]

He also asked prospective jurors if they had an "orthodox religion," like the Second Vatical Council. One juror replied he was "more conservative than that."

He also asked if there were any educators in the room, and "...if children aren't properly socialized, can they be socially stunted in the way they interact with people?"

He asked one educator if a child could be "brainwashed."

"Yes," the prospective juror answered, especially at a "young age"

"Is there anybody here who thinks brainwashing is voodoo, or fake or made up or stuff that defense attorneys like me kind of raise in cases?"

---

50. Manuscript of jury trial, Vol. 2, April 8, 2024.

There was no response.

"… is anybody familiar with any cults, or some of you guys watch … true crime stuff?" Anybody familiar with stuff like that? Can you have cult-like behavior in families?"

"Yes," one person answered.

He also asked if anyone was familiar with the Stockholm Syndrome.

"I believe it was the kidnapping scenario and it's when the victims end up like their captors and sympathize with them," one person replied.

"Okay. And is that a form of basically brainwashing?"

"It could be, yes."

After the group was sent out of the courtroom, the attorneys began striking some and accepting others before settling on six jurors and two alternates.

Camuccio would later say that he had one overriding question. "Can they listen to the experts but get through the B.S.?"[51]

---

51. Interview with Camuccio, June 6, 2025.

CHAPTER 15

OPENING SALVO

"Opening statement is the lawyer's first opportunity to obtain a substantive edge on the opponent. In the battle of strategy, evidence, and demonstration, the opening statement can create momentum out of the gate that sets the tone for the entire case."[52]

Assistant State Attorney Tom Weczorek led off the trial with the opening statement for the state.

"Over the next several days you all are going to learn about the circumstances surrounding the death, the murder of Sue-Ellen Anselmo on March 13, 2019, in the Greenwood Cemetery in Eustis, Florida at the hands of her stepson, Ian Anselmo, the defendant in this case."[53]

"...you will learn these facts in several different ways. You will learn the facts of the case through the testimony of eyewitnesses who responded to Greenwood Cemetery and found Sue-Ellen lifeless, slumped over in her vehicle. You

---

52. Spencer Lucas, "Opening Statement: Creating a Competitive Advantage," *Advocate* magazine, January 2015.
53. Trial Transcript, April 9, 2004.

are going to learn the facts of the case of reviewing bodycam camera worn by the officers who initially responded to Greenwood Cemetery when Sue-Ellen was killed."

He continued mentioning the long list of evidence, including Ian's 911 call, crime scene photos, autopsy pictures, and physical evidence such as the phone cord and bloody clothing.

He said they also would be "introduced" to the Anselmos.

No one could criticize the assistant state attorney's presentation as sensational. "The Anselmo family was fairly tight knit," he said dryly.

It would be a big contrast to the more colorful statements to follow by Hornsby. The question would be, would the jury like the "just the facts ma'am" approach better?[54]

Jurors, generally, seem to like the "facts are stubborn things" argument.

He talked about Dejah leaving the family, why, and how the family cut ties.

"But in February of 2019, Dejah-Thoris wanted to have contact with her mother and wanted to share with her mother essentially how good [her] life was going, how successful she had become both personally and professionally. And Dejah-Thoris wanted to explain to her mother why she decided that she could no longer live in the same home...."

He detailed how Sue-Ellen left John, taking five children with her and moving into Dejah's house. "And over the next week, John Anselmo waged a campaign against his wife,

---

54. Catch phrase used by fictional detective Joe Friday on the *Dragnet* TV series.

Sue-Ellen, to try to get her return to the house and return the five to him."

He talked about why Rajko was returned to his father, and how she finally agreed to meet with Ian, "with whom Sue-Ellen had had, at least recently, a fairly good relationship…."

"And for reasons that are unknown the two of them proceeded into Greenwood Cemetery in Eustis, not far from the Anselmo's house."

He promised them that they would see body-worn camera footage as well as photographs showing blood on Ian Anselmo's hands. And they would also witness Ian Anselmo telling law enforcement that he's so sorry and that his father was going to be so mad, he said.

In his most graphic statement, he said: "You'll have an opportunity to see Sue-Ellen's lifeless body in the driver's seat of the vehicle. When she's initially found, she is sort of leaning back into the rear passenger compartment of the vehicle. There is a maroon phone cord draped over her left shoulder and she's lifeless. And initially law enforcement checking for a pulse could not find one. And she's obviously very injured and you can see the injury to her face; you can see the blood."

He promised jurors, "…the state of Florida is going to present to you the facts of Sue-Ellen Anselmo's death. The facts which prove beyond a reasonable doubt that the defendant Ian Anselmo is legally responsible for his stepmother's murder.

"If the defense chooses to present the case to you, I expect you may hear evidence in the form of opinion testimony which will try to essentially negate the defendant's responsibility for his mother's death."

Some of the state's witnesses will offer opinions, too, he said, the medical examiner, for example, and criminologists from the crime lab.

He said they could end up believing 100 percent of the expert's testimony, 50 percent, or none of it. "You are the finders of fact."

He said, "The state will prove that Ian Anselmo murdered his mother and her unborn child, and that his actions were "done out of hatred, ill-will, spite and evil intentions." He knew the consequences and knew that his actions were wrong.

Hornsby began his opening statement by referring to Wieczorek's use of the word "facts."

"...usually when attorneys stress a specific word, they're trying to develop a theme. And frankly, I think in this case you're gonna be asking yourself, well, that's a fact, it is a fact of that person. And trying to think when I was thinking about this case, what was going to be my opening statement? What's my opinion of this case? How do I explain this to you? How do I explain that a stepson strangled his own stepmother?"

Wieczorek's opening statement was "a very sterile explanation to this case," he said.

"Is this like *Alice in Wonderland* where up is down and down is up? Is this like the inmates' jail where we have an extreme patriarch relationship where everybody else is subservient to the patriarch? Is this a cult?

"You know, a cult admits to made-up missions and they all seem to have very similar things. A cult's defined as excessive adoration or devotion to a particular person. It's a misplaced adoration or devotion to a particular person. It's a misplaced exaggerated adoration for a particular reason. The system of veneration, devotion, directed toward a particular figure or object.

"If I had to tell you that there was going to be a particular theme that you will see developed in this case, I would say that you will believe that this family had become a cult. Not because of Ian. Ian was part of the cult, the personality. The cult's personality surrounding the central figures in this entire case, whether he wants to be or not.

"And I'm gonna tell you right, Mr. Camuccio in his closing arguments will say this case is not about John Anselmso. And pragmatically I agree with him. But this case is about John Anselmo. That's the truth.

"And make no mistake, I don't disagree with, as Mr. Wieczorek called them, the facts. You will see bodycam graphics. There will be no doubt that Ian Anselmo strangled his stepmother. There will be no doubt that he called the police. None of that's in dispute.

"But how does someone get there? Sometimes the *how* is as important as *what*. So, I'm going to try to give you the same explanation as Mr. Wieczorek did, but fill in, I guess what we'll call the juicy part of the story, about this cult's personality that is surrounded by the man John Anselmo."

Hornsby told the jurors that they will probably look at each other and think, "there is no way what he's saying is truthful." However, because of the cult personality, the family members will believe it to be true.

"The state's own expert described it as they were brainwashed. I believe one of the state's first witnesses will say that she was brainwashed."

He said it would become clear that the children were "conditioned" to have absolute devotion, first to John, and then to the family."

He said John's biological children would be fed "delusional" beliefs about how they were kidnapped by their biological mother, and all of them would be told that Sue-Ellen was guilty of infidelity and substance abuse.

John would reinforce this belief and it would have a devastating effect psychologically, creating a fear of being kidnapped at any moment, Hornsby said.

He said John and Sue-Ellen's marriage was normal at first but changed over time, with John accusing her of cheating on him and abusing substances. He said they would hear how "… he made Sue-Ellen stop cutting men's hair. He made her start dressing more modestly. He made her where she basically had to come directly back home all the time. She stopped being allowed to go out with her friends. She started becoming isolated from basically her prior life.

"You will hear from Sue-Ellen's biological daughter and strangely, Sue-Ellen's biological daughter refers to Mr. Anselmo as her father when I spoke to her earlier after this case, and I assume she still does. And she's gonna tell you that these children lived an extremely isolated and abusive life. The conditions, she described it as like training a dog."

He said they would hear about their little church, how Dejah ran away to live with her grandparents, and how Dejah's life was so traumatic she considered suicide.

He said Dejah was on the outs with the "Anselmo Code," which he described as a "Sicilian Mafia-like devotion to John Anselmo."

The children were not allowed to have any friends. "They never left the house. They didn't watch like *Transformers* or *G.I. Joe* or something like that, they watched stuff like Bob Hope. They watched Mr. Wiggles. Fifteen and 16-year-old kids are watching stuff like Mr. Wiggles.

They had a sterilized exposure to society. They had beyond an unsure understanding of society. And they were kept completely isolated from society."

He mentioned Rajko's attempt to strangle Sue-Ellen before Ian strangled her, and the confrontation in the cemetery when Dejah invited Sue-Ellen's friends to bring flowers.

Hornsby said during the fateful last week of Sue-Ellen's life the children were "constantly on edge" because of the things John was telling them.

He said Ian had been medicated and "managed" since 2010. "You will find that about everybody in the family is mentally ill." There is a genetic propensity for mental illness, he explained.

He said Ian suffered from major depressive disorder, and when his prescription drug schedule was disrupted, he would suffer from antidepressive withdrawal syndrome and that it would be a contributing factor to temporary insanity.

In what Hornsby called "uncontroverted testimony," he said that when Sue-Ellen left on that Wednesday, she took Ian's medication (he would later say John could have taken it, but it didn't matter).

He laid out what his defense experts would conclude.

"Now, there are a few things that are odds and ends that I just want to tell you about because you'll hear about it. I like to tell you about everything up front. So, when you hear something during the trial and you're like, oh, Mr. Hornsby didn't say that, why was he trying to hide that?

"You're gonna hear some other things that the family may or may not believe," he said, adding, "everybody will agree that Ian was a child trapped in a man's body. You'll see pictures of his bedroom. To this day, he still has hundreds of toys in his room. You're gonna hear that his entire life he's talked to his toys, two in particular, that he named Slash and Puppy. You'll hear that when he wrote letters to Mr. Anselmo from jail he said, 'hug Slash and Puppy for me.'

"You'll hear from the doctors that these are signs of a schizoaffective disorder." He said it was "not quite schizophrenia" but there are similar "overlapping conditions."

He described Ian as "childish," yet he has a genius IQ. That he was an aspiring wrestler and fascinated with the "fantasy world" of the sport, wanting to be the hero character in the ring.

He and Sue-Ellen bonded over his desire to be a professional wrestler, Hornsby said.

"He is an aspiring writer but his writing is always limited to communicate with people from his home."

He talked about the state's expert witness, Dr. Tania Werner.

"She's gonna give an opinion. And you'll find that actually she's testified for Mr. Camuccio in other cases about insanity. And surprisingly, she doesn't believe it occurred in those cases. You're gonna find my guy's testified for other people, as well.

"But it's just their opinion. But when you look at the totality, at the end of the day you make that decision, right?

"And because she said well, I don't believe he was insane at the time, you look at everything. You're going to go back there and you're gonna feel sorry for Sue-Ellen. And I did. You're gonna feel sorry for probably everybody that's in this family. You're probably gonna be most upset at John. You're gonna be upset with Ian. But you will see that he was a mental head case that had a combustible event that resulted in this dissociative event.

"And the only explanation for it is when he's medicated, he's fine. When he's not put in these chaotic situations, everything, at least in this world, is fine. And because of that, I'm asking you, when you see all of this that you return a verdict of not guilty by reason of insanity. After you hear this story, you're definitely gonna believe it's crazy."

CHAPTER 16

DEJAH TAKES THE STAND

Dejah was the first witness to take the stand, which was fitting since it was her anguished, courageous letter to her mother that set things in motion.

Camuccio led her through the basics: That she was the biological daughter of Sue-Ellen, that Ian was her stepbrother, he was one month older and that she and her mother joined the family when she was seven years old. He also had her identify Ian sitting at the defense table.

"He's wearing a striped shirt and a gray tie."

The prosecutor had a clear goal: Keep the focus on Ian as much as possible. Dejah's testimony would be valuable, he figured, if she talked about his intelligence, that Sue-Ellen was afraid of him, and if she could pour cold water on the theory that Sue-Ellen took Ian's medications with her when she left.

"At some point, were you guys going to public school?" Camuccio asked.

"Yes,"

"Would you go to the same school together?"

"We did."

"Same grade?"

"Yes."

"And is he intelligent?"

"Yes."

"And when I say intelligent, is he highly intelligent?"

"Vey. Highly intelligent."

She identified John as her "stepdad," though within a few minutes she would say that he had adopted her.

She said John and her mother were together less than a year before they married.

"At some point did you leave the residence?"

"Yes, I did."

"And how old were you then?"

"I was 18."

"Now, I want to go back to February or March 2019. Did there come a time that you sent a letter to your mother about allegations you were making against John Anselmo?"

"Yes."

"And without getting into detail about what those allegations were, did they involve physical or sexual abuse against you by John Anselmo?"

"Both, yes."

Camuccio had to bring up the allegations to set up the timeline, but avoided getting into the details, keeping the focus on Ian.

"Now, after receiving that letter, did Sue-Ellen come stay with you?"

"Yes, she did."

"And about how long was it from the time that you sent the letter to her that she was able to get over to your residence?"

"About two to three weeks."

"And during that time, were you aware that Sue-Ellen was making attempts to basically start a divorce proceeding?"

"Yes. We had a civil assist, so we had a police officer accompany us to the house to make sure that we were not in danger."

"Was Sue-Ellen in fear at that point?"

"She was, yes."

She recounted going to the Anselmo home and how John and Ian were away at a wrestling training facility in Orlando.

"Was there a particular reason why it was chosen to do it when they would have been at wrestling school?"

"Yes. My mother was afraid of Johnny and Ian."

She said they gathered up the five biological children her mother shared with John.

"They came into the car just fine with me and my husband and they listened to my mother.," she said.

She said John and Ian contacted Sue-Elleno "multiple times a day" about bringing the children back.

The day the children were removed, she said Johnny came to her house. "And there was a lot of banging on the door, a lot of shouting outside."

Police, who had been advised of the situation beforehand, arrived.

Camuccio asked her if she had a chance to go through the belongings that her mother had brought to her house.

She said she did.

"And as you were going through her belongings, did you ever find anything that belonged to Ian Anselmo when you went through everything?"

"I did not."

"Specifically, did you ever find any medications that belonged to Ian Anselmo when you went through all of the belongings your mother left behind?"

"I did not."

Hornsby, of course, had a much different agenda. His job was to present his theory of the case: Ian was temporarily insane because of his bizarre, torturous, cultish upbringing and because he was without his medication, which led to a psychotic break. He saw, after taking her deposition, that Sue-Ellen would be a likeable, credible witness to surviving life with John Anselmo.

Hornsby asked many questions on cross-examination, starting with her middle name, Chloe.

"And at some point, John Anselmo adopted you; is that correct?"

"Yes."

"When did that happen?"

"I think I was 13."

"Okay, and at some point, he had your name changed, correct?"

"Yes."

"And he selected Dejah-Thoris, right?

"Yes. My mother and him jointly."

"Okay. And Dejah-Thoris, what is that after?"

"John Carter, Edgar Rice Burroughs. It's a book character. Dejah-Thoris is the Princes Warrior of Mars."

Okay. And that sounds like something that would be Mr. Anselmo's idea, right?"

"My mother was a big reader as well, so both of them."

"Okay. And I don't know how you stand today, but at least, we've met previously on one occasion, correct?"

"Yes."

"And at least at that time, which was a little over a year after your mother's passing, or maybe you still referred to Mr. Anselmo as your father, right?"

"I did at the time."

"Okay. And that's changed now?"

"He is still my stepdad but I call him Johnny now."

"Right, because now you obviously do not have that …."

"Emotional attachment."

He brought up the fact that she and Ian were together "24/7," as he put it. "And you were basically best friends in the household?"

"Yes"

He then took her through the first few "normal" years of her mother's marriage to John in 2005, and how Sue-Ellen changed from being an independent, "sociable person" after a couple of years.

"...she dressed how she wanted, right?"

"Yes."

"Once things started to change did John start becoming paranoid?"

"Yes."

She dressed more conservatively, he refused to let her cut men's hair and was more controlling, she said.

"... did it get to the point where you started being expected to care for the children as if you were their caregiver while your mother worked?"

"Yes."

"And would your father use that against Sue-Ellen?"

"Yes."

"And would he actually pit or try to make her feel bad for ... working and [not] caring for the children?"

"Yes."

"And would he also pit the children against each other?"

"Yes."

He asked her if she thought the way he was doing things was normal, or that he led her to believe it was normal.

"Yes, I did believe it."

"And so, when he would punish you, he would make you do things such as push-ups until exhaustion?"

"Yes.

"Squatting until you collapsed."

"Yes."

"Waking you up in the middle of the night and making you work out until you couldn't move anymore?"

"Yes."

"How old were you at that point?"

"Eight, nine. Once we hit double digits it became more physical."

"… how would he physically – I use this word loosely – punish you?"

"Head-butting, kicking, pulling of the hair."

"And was it the same for other children?"

"It was, yes."

He would hit the boys harder and longer, she said.

"Okay, and what would happen if you were defiant towards him? If, say, I'll use the example I think you used before, he slapped you and you didn't cry?

"He would slap harder."

"Until what?"

"Until you showed that it hurt."

"And so, the way he acted was almost as if he was training a dog, correct?"

"Correct."

She talked about how punishment included being forced to sleep on the garage floor.

"Was this a nice garage?"

"No. Concrete floors, no lights, spiders, cockroaches."

What would he do with the boys?"

"They would sleep outside, regardless of the weather."

She said there were concerns that John might kill Eric, so he was separated."

"He would be brought upstairs and away," she said.

He also asked, "What is the Anselmo code?"

"You don't say anything that's been in the house to anybody else."

"And if you leave the Anselmo family, are you basically ostracized?"

"Yes"

"And you believed it to be similar to like a Sicilian or Mafia loyalty, is that correct?"

"Correct."

"Based upon your experience, now having been outside of the family, did you find it to be an abnormal, let me see what you said."

"Yes."

"I think you used the word paranoia, right?"

"Right".

"Okay. Would anybody ever cross the line with John in your family?"

"No."

"Did anybody try?"

"We didn't really want to find out what happened."

"Okay. So, everybody was basically too scared to?"

"Right."

She said she ran away when she was 18.

Hornsby asked about the family's 20-member church. When he asked if it was conservative, she said it was "much more" than the current church theology. He went so far to compare it to *The Hand Maiden's Tale*, where women are subservient to men.

"Heard of it," she said.

"At the time … you were basically the one, and I believe it was with Ian's help, raising these children, right?"

"Correct."

"Korak, it was to such an extent that Korak thought you were his mother, right?"

"Not that he thought I was his mother, but I was his caretaker. I was closest to him."

"But you consider him basically to be your baby, right?"

"I do, yes."

"Okay. Because your mother, and I'm not faulting your mother, she was the one that would go out and work, and have to work all day and then come home, right?"

"She was the breadwinner, yes."

"And in normal circumstances, the breadwinner isn't generally expected to also have to be the house maker and home caregiver?"

"Correct."

"And I'm not disagreeing with you on that. I'm not trying to fault your mother. I'm just trying to understand that. But the problem was though that John forced this responsibility onto the older children rather than himself?"

"Correct."

"Okay. And so, once you started getting home schooling, you guys never had any friends, right?"

"Right."

"No one ever came over?"

"Nope."

"Never went over and stayed over at anybody's house?"

"No."

"Neer had any, in your regard, boyfriends, right?"

"No. Correct."

"The kids never had any girlfriends – I mean the boys never had any girlfriends?"

"Correct."

"They thought things as simple as getting to go to the store with a parent was like a big deal, right?"

"Correct."

"Now that you've been outside, is that a big deal?"

"No."

"That's just a normal routine activity, right?"

"Right."

"The shows that you guys were allowed to watch were limited, right?"

"Correct."

"You had to watch like shows that involved, you know, olden styled comedy like Bob Hope and things of that nature, right?"

"Correct."

"The cartoons that the kids had to watch were stuff like Mr. Wiggles (*The Wiggles*), right?"

"Correct."

"And they watched those even until past the natural or normal age for a child to watch those?"

"Up to when I left at 18."

"And you now agree that that's bizarre, right? And that's all the socializing all your siblings had was this type of upraising within the household?"

"Correct."

"And again, I don't mean to keep coming back to this, this ultimate thing, but at the time you left, you still thought that was all normal?"

"Correct."

"And it took years after your mother's passing to really, I guess, as you said, break the emotional bond and realize that that's not normal?"

"Correct."

"Okay. And was breaking that emotional bond like being able to stop calling John Anselmo 'Dad' and start referring to him as Johnny, as I think you do now? Did that take a lot of internal strength on your part to reach that point?"

"Yes."

"And even though Ian caused your mother's passing, you believe the catalyst was John, right?"

"Yes."

"And that's even with that belief, you still had that bond with Johnny Anselmo, right? By calling him Dad, right? Let me rephrase it. Remember when we last talked, you said that he so conditioned you that you felt he would, and if you don't remember this tell me, but that he trained you to forget the bad things and only remember the good things that happened?"

"That's correct."

"And so, because of that, the years of conditioning, it took you a long time to be able to break that, that conditioning that he had done so that you no longer thought of him as 'Dad' and thought of him as a separate person?"

"Correct."

"Thank you. Now, your first exposure, aside from in sixth grade when you stopped going to elementary school, your first exposure to the outside world was when you started to go to Lake-Sumter Community College, right?"

"Correct."

"But how did you get there every day?"

"My father drove me.

"And your father, you mean, John"

"Yes."

"So, he would drive you there every day. And did you have rules for when you would go there?"

"Yes. I was not allowed to leave the building in any way."

He asked if she had been "exposed to someone that said, 'Hey, that is not normal.'"

"Yes, I did."

"And then did that pique your interest, or get you realizing that this isn't normal life/"

"It did."

The real trouble, she said, was when she wanted to go to the library and start dating a young man.

John's reaction?

"He physically hurt me very badly."

"And do you think it's because … John viewed you as, for lack of a better term, as his property?"

"Yes,"

"And so, you weren't allowed to date other men?"

"I was not"

"Okay. And because of that, you got physically punished?"

"Yes."

He had her tell how she skateboarded to her grandparents' home when she ran away. Only John and Sue-Ellen had drivers licenses in the home.

She said she made an effort to memorize the route. The house is only five minutes away.

"Did that go over well with John?"

"No, it did not."

"What happened?"

"My mother showed up at the house and my, John called and asked me to come home. She asked why I was leaving. John was very matter of fact. He just said, 'Are you really gonna do this? Come back home. We're not going to do this right now.'"

"Okay. At some point did they try to use your bond with Korak as basically leverage to force you to come back?"

"They did, yes."

"And if you had gone back because of Korak, do you feel like you would have been able to leave again?"

"I do not. That's why I didn't go."

"Okay. So, you knew no matter how much you loved Korak that if you went back, you were going to be trapped again?"

"Correct."

"All right. Now, you understand that he's (Ian)}been seeing (psychiatrist) Dr. DeLeon for a long time, right?"

"Yes."

"And whenever he or anybody was taken to Dr. DeLeon, John took them, right?"

"Correct."

"And in the last, I guess years before you left, Ian's behavior had suddenly changed?"

"Yes."

"Okay. He had become, I guess, more withdrawn or more antisocial toward your older siblings?"

"Correct."

"And he was like a child in a man's body, correct?"

"Yes."

Hornsby then turned to the notion that Ian talked to his toys. Dejah's testimony took a bit of an unexpected turn, but he was still able to make a point.

"And Ian had his room; do you remember his room, did he have toys all over the room?"

"Yes."

"Even until, and I guess at the time you left, he would also been about 18, right?"

"Correct."

"And Ian had a pet, a toy named Slash that he would talk to?"

"I don't know about talked to, but he did have a toy Slash, yes."

"Okay. And what about a toy, I guess a stuffed animal maybe, Puppy?"

"We all did."

"Okay. So, and you have to understand, this is a different situation than a normal case because we, well, I agree, this is abnormal for you, you had your own, I guess, characters that you talked to, right?"

"I did, yes."

"And probably the reason for this is because you didn't have any friends, right, to confide in?

"Yes."

"And as you talked to anybody in your family about some, you know, personal feelings…."

"You had to confide in them, that they wouldn't say something," she said.

"But you were afraid they would say something, right?"

"Correct."

"So you were always on edge that you couldn't say, hey, this is abnormal, there's something wrong, so you would have these pet whatever things that we all have?"

"Yes."

Hornsby moved on to what he called "the deal" that John made with Dejah.

"The deal was that if I joined the Air Force, I was allowed to have contact with my younger siblings."

"And at that time, was it gut-wrenching for you not to be able to have contact with your younger siblings?"

"Extremely, yes."

"And so had you ever thought about going into the military before this?"

"Never. "Before I even got shipped out to basic, he had already recanted the deal."

The deal was a six-year contract that was canceled when she received a medical discharge after just a few months.

Hornsby led her, not just through the physical abuse of the children, but also the emotional toll of the individuals and the omnipresent risk of suicide.

"...the medications in its way kept some of the kids in like a zombie-like stage, right?"

"Correct."

She testified about trying to reach out to her mother and receiving texts from her phone.

"But you didn't believe they were from your mother?"

"Right."

"Who were they from?"

"Johnny."

"Okay. And how could you tell?"

"The way it was written. She did later confirm when she came to my house before the attack."

"At one point was John engaged in, I guess, what you would call unexpected stalking behavior?"

"Yes."

"Can you give me some examples?"

"He followed my husband around while were dating."

"And how would he have even known that you were dating this person after you left?"

"He always knew everything."

"Okay."

"I honestly don't always know how."

"Okay. Fair enough. But he was still present in your life even after you had not only left, but supposedly had been ostracized from the family, right?"

"Yes."

'And if you would ask your mother to meet for lunch, were there times when you tried to ask your mother for lunch and....?

"There was, yes."

"And then what happened? And did he start attacking you for trying to separate them or something?"

"I got a text from John asking why I was trying to get my mother alone."

She said there was no way she could reach her siblings, because they did not have phones or email addresses.

"What kind of phone was in the house?"

"We had a flip phone that just had one through nine numbers with an answer button and a hang-up button."

Her mother's phone had text capability, she said.

"And so, even after you left, John was still controlling you?"

"Yes,"

"And he controlled all the kids, correct?"

"Correct."

"And he controlled Sue-Ellen?"

"Yes."

"And in the letter, in addition to revealing the sexual assault that you said was inflicted on you, you also informed your mother she was worth more, right?"

"Yes."

"That she was actually right about John brainwashing, I guess, everyone?"

"Yes."

"And that the kids don't deserve to get hit?"

"Yes."

Even after Dejah and her mother reconnected before she left John, Dejah said she felt lucky if she could talk to her twice a day.

"That should be normal behavior, right?"

"Right."

Hornsby then switched to questions about Rajko, that John created homicidal tendencies in his young, impressionable children.

"Rajko was your mother's first child with John, right?

"Correct."

"And he was considered the golden child in the family, right?"

"Right"

"Did he sleep in his own room or where did he sleep?"

"He slept with John."

"In the same bed?"

"Yes."

"And where did Sue-Ellen sleep?"

"The sleeping situation changed many times in the house," she said. Sometimes he (John) slept on the couch with one of the children, sometimes he kicked her out of her bed to sleep. "I've slept with my mom in the regular bed," she said. "But John always slept with Rajko.

"And you agree that once you get past the toddler age, it's not really normal ….?"

"Correct."

Hornsby then led her through what he called Rajko "basically mimicking" John when he tried to strangle his mother with a blanket one night shortly after she moved out.

"Sue-Ellen called John and asked if he would say goodnight to the children and that they would talk in the morning, and let the children get some sleep," she said.

"Real calm, kind of normal stuff, right?"

"Yes."

"Was his response calm and normal?"

"It was not."

"Can you describe it to the jury?"

"John started yelling at Rajko that he needs to run away, he needs to get out, do anything he can. Get out of the house. It was …."

"And how…?"

"…exaggerated."

"What kind of effect did this have on Rajko?"

"He became exaggerated. He told John the only reason he wasn't killing my mother was because she had a baby in her belly. He grabbed a flashlight; he wanted to hit her."

"And at some point, your mother tries to calm Rajko down?"

"Yes."

Dejah said the two were in a bedroom, and she had left.

"And did you hear a commotion?"

"Yes."

"And what happens when you come back in because of the commotion?"

"Rajko had a sheet wrapped around my mother's neck."

"And what was he trying to do?"

"He was trying to pull as hard as he could."

"So, he was trying to strangle her?"

"Correct."

"And I believe he's a 10-year-old kid at the time?"

"Yes."

"And this is how strong his bond is with his….?"

"With John."

"…his father that he is trying to strangle his own biological mother?"

"Yes."

"Clearly he had been brainwashed, right?"

"Correct."

"And so, what did you endeavor to do?"

"We decided to take Rajko back to John,"

Hornsby asked if there was anything or anyone in the house that posed a danger to the children and she said no.

"And after you left, John obviously became more strict, more paranoid, more severe on the family, correct?"

"Right."

"And the children basically mimicked the belief system that John had instilled in them, right?"

"Right."

He asked if Ian was in a "manic state" that week.

"I do not know. I only got text messages.... I got the impression he was very upset."

"Okay. Okay. But during this time, John had essentially lost control of the family, right?"

"Yes."

"Now, he was freaking out, right?"

"Yes."

"And when John freaks out, it affects the children, right?"

"Yes."

He asked her if what he said to the children was so "over the top" that they had a "heightened sense of extremes."

She agreed that was the case.

Hornsby, referring to the fact that the children were only exposed to "basically children's TV shows," commented that "none of the children were ever raised to actually grow up, it was like they were Peter Pan, right?"

"Correct."

Hornsby then talked about the violent confrontation that Nico and Rajko had with Dejah at her mother's gravesite.

"And at this time, you had actually gotten a restraining order against John, right?"

"Yes."

"I think that was because he had confronted you at the hospital where your mother was?"

"Correct."

She recalled leaving the cemetery briefly, then returning to find Nico and Rajko "kicking, hollering" and trying to destroy the flowers adorning the grave.

"And John was off basically as an overseer far enough away not to violate the injunction?"

"Correct."

She said Nico pulled her down, grabbed her hair and tried choking her.

"And did she seem to be in her right mind when she was doing this?"

"No."

"You're trying to reason with her while she's trying to choke you and she's not in reality, is she?"

"She would pause momentarily and tell me what I was saying couldn't be true."

"Okay. Because she had been brainwashed, right?"

"Yes."

"And you turned to John and you said something to him?

"Yes."

"What did you say?"

"I said, 'You're just gonna sit there and watch them,' something along those lines, 'and not do anything?' She also said that I killed my mother by taking her off of life support. And I looked at Johnny and said, 'Is this what you're telling them?'"

"Because that wasn't true?"

"That was not true."

"And at the same time, Rajko's kicking people, right?"

"Yes."

"And so, these kids are acting like the trained dogs they had become, right?"

"Yes."

"And when you were in that family you felt you were conditioned the same way to an extreme, right?"

"Right."

"Is your mother still buried at Greenwood Cemetery?"

"No."

"What happened?"

"He dug her back up and cremated her."

"And that's, in your mind problematic for what reason?"

"So that I no longer have a grave to visit or flowers to bring"

"And does that also run afoul of your religious beliefs?"

"It did, yes."

"And why is that?"

"As a Catholic, you're not supposed to do any harm to the body, such as cremation."

"Because you can't rise from your death, right?"

"Right."

On redirect, Camuccio asked what form of Catholicism she was referring to.

She explained that it was Sedevacantism.

"And part of that training and upbringing would have been for all the children?"

"Correct"

"Including Ian?"

"Correct."

"Does that include the Ten Commandments?

"It does, yes."

"Does that include, "Thou shall not kill?"

"It does, yes."

"Nothing further."

CHAPTER 17

THE DEAD GIVE UP THEIR SECRETS

In 1999, I received a call from a trusted source. "I thought you might want to know," the tipster said. "The Mount Dora Police Department has classified a homicide as natural. That's not right. This is murder."[55]

The scenic, tourist favorite Lake County city was suffering a black eye after a series of violent crimes, including the home invasion murder of an elderly man whose throat had been cut.

Now, another elderly man had been found dead under suspicious circumstances. A knife and a pillow were found beside the 85-year-old's body, and there were signs of a break-in. However, police didn't share that information with the medical examiner, who was only told that he had a bad heart. The pathologist only performed an external examination.

I wrote a series of investigative stories about it in the *Orlando Sentinel* until pressured authorities exhumed the body for

---

55. Frank Stanfield, *Vampires, Gators and Wackos, A Florida Newspaperman's Life*, WildBlue Press, 2022.

a full autopsy. His pacemaker was removed and sent it to the manufacturer. The data proved he had been suffocated, apparently by the pillow, the pathologist concluded.

Confronted with the evidence, the 16-year-old killer confessed and he was convicted of second-degree murder.

Not every case is as dramatic as that one. In fact, because Sue-Ellen's homicide was not a whodunit, her autopsy was not expected to be crucial, but for legal reasons there had to be testimony about the examination. Ultimately, it was both telling and sad.

Dr. Shandelle Norford was an assistant medical examiner in Orlando when she performed the autopsy. Norford, who is board certified in three different areas of pathology, owned a consulting firm by the time she testified in the Anselmo case.

Camuccio took her through the basics: what pathologists look for, how they perform an autopsy, and how they view collateral information, which in Sue-Ellen's case were hospital records.

Included in her report was the sentence: "The body is that of a well-developed, well-nourished, 68-inch, 159 lb. woman who appears the reported age of 39 years."[56]

Personal effects were listed as a necklace with pendant and cross and rosary beads.

"Now, when you did your review of her medical records, did you find any other injuries to the face area that would not have been seen in the external examination?" Camuccio asked.[57]

---

56. ME 2019 – 00453 Postmortem Examination of the Body of Sue-Ellen Anselmo. March 19, 2019.
57. Trial transcript, Vol IV, April 9, 2024.

"Sure. The medical records outline the fracture of the angle of the left jaw."

Camuccio then showed her a series of photographs and asked her to explain images of facial injuries.

"There were some superficial injuries to the cheeks. There was bruising and some abrasions, just superficial cuts to the chin and jaw area. There was also some bruising, extensive bruising, on the neck, on the anterior and the left and right side of the neck.".

In preparing to show her another photograph, he asked her to define a "pattern injury."

"So, pattern injury is something that you can identify. We call it something like irregular patterns. They align, the checkered pattern. It's something that's identifiable."

Camuccio noted that the autopsy was performed a week after the attack. "So would looking at crime scene photos that show her injuries at the time also help explain the injuries that ultimately led to her death?"

"Yes, that would be very helpful," she said.

"So, I am seeing two patterns here that is consistent with, I would say, a ligature compression on the neck, as well las manual strangulation, using your hands as well."

"…the injuries that you're seeing, would that be necessarily consistent with, well, what if someone was strangling somebody and the cord just happened to be there, would you still see that ligature mark, that red, that deep in that scenario?"

"No, because in order to see a bruise in this case, you have to have pressure applying to damage the underlying blood vessels."

As part of the autopsy, pathologists remove the scalp from the skull. By doing so, the examiner can see hemorrhage or bruising underneath the skin, she said.

"And in this case, she did have some bleeding underneath in the scalp," she said before pointing out three places in a photo where there was evidence of bleeding.

"And what is this area over here?" Camuccio asked, pointing to a photograph.

"This is the temporalis muscle."

The temporalis muscle, sometimes called the temporal muscle, is a fan-shaped muscle used in chewing and biting.

"And is there injury to that as well?"

"There was bleeding under the scalp, we have injury to the muscles. That is typically some kind of like blunt force injury or trauma." There were injuries to both the left and right side.

Camuccio asked her to give her opinion on the cause of death.

"The ultimate cause of death was strangulation."

"...as part of your autopsy did you also discover evidence that she was, in fact, pregnant?"

"... she had an enlarged uterus, which I opened, and inside the uterus was an embryonic sac with some fluid housing a baby inside."

The baby was still alive at the time Sue-Ellen was admitted to the hospital, according to hospital records, she said.

Camuccio asked her the medical term for strangulation.

"So, on the death certificate, I had anoxic encephalopathy due to cardiopulmonary arrest, which is strangulation. Anoxic encephalopathy, meaning brain injury, that happened as a result of lack of oxygen to the brain from the strangulation."

Apply enough pressure, and you compress the structures in the neck and you block the airway, depriving blood and oxygen from going to the brain, she said.

"Now, during your review of the evidence in this case, were there indications that there was a struggle prior to Sue-Ellen's death?"

She said there was. "In this case, there were so many irregular markings in the neck, going up to the chin, as well as irregular markings on the cheek. You also see deep hemorrhage inside the muscles of the neck as well, under four different layers."

"So, this was not an instantaneous event?"

"Correct."

"The manner of death is a homicide," she said.

Hornsby on cross-examination asked which came first, the ligature or the manual strangulation marks.

She said it was hard to say.

He then asked if it was possible that the cord could get caught up beneath his hands, which would account for two patterns.

"You know, in this case, to see that linear pattern, it takes a lot of force."

"And so, you would expect to see corresponding indentations on his hands, I would say, right?"

"I mean, not necessarily, because the force is applied to the neck, not your hands."

That was the end of the questioning. Not mentioned was a portion of the autopsy report entitled "identifying marks and scars."

It stated: "A monochromatic tattoo of non-English characters is on the right hip. A monochromatic insignia "JOHNNY'S GIRL" is on the upper aspect of the left buttock."

CHAPTER 18

"WHAT DID YOU DO?"

John's character lurked like a dark cloud against the backdrop of witness testimony, and Hornsby made sure it stayed that way.

Eustis Police Detective Chris Horst, who was the lead investigator, took the stand to testify about his involvement in the case.

"On Marh 13, 2019, at approximately 4:08 p.m., I was actually about to leave, and I heard over the radio that we got a call of a homicide."[58]

Camuccio had him point out on a display board where the cemetery was located, where the attack took place, and where the Anselmo home is located, "Actually, just around the corner."

Camuccio then asked Horst about inmate calls from the county jail. It immediately became apparent why the questions were relevant.[59]

---

58. Trial transcript, Vol. IV, April 9, 2024.
59. This conversation was edited to eliminate the "F-bombs."

"This is a free call from Ian Anselmo," the automated voice noted. "An inmate at Lake County Detention Center. This call is subject to recording and monitoring. To accept this free call, press 1. To refuse this free call press two. Thank you for using Securus. You may start the conversation now."

Ian: "Hello?"

John: "What the [expletive] did you do?"

Ian: "I just (indiscernible)."

John: "I'm in the hospital right now in ORMC [Orlando Regional Medical Center]. She's gonna die."

Ian: (crying).

John: "What did you do?"

Ian: (crying).

John: "I'm so pissed off at you! "I'm so ... (indiscernible). I don't know why you did this. I don't know why you did this."

Ian: (crying).

John: "I don't understand anything you're saying,"

Ian: "I'm sorry. I miss you so much (indiscernible).

John: "I don't understand what you're saying."

Ian: "She's been ruining the family so much (indiscernible) everything. I don't know why I did it."

John: "But you, you're not supposed to do that."

Ian: "I know. That's why it's so hard.

John: "I don't like (indiscernible). I cannot be crying in the middle of the ... (indiscernible) right now."

Ian: "I love you."

John: "I love you, too, Ian. But what the …. I know you were sad but you can't (Indiscernible) … crazy."

Ian: "It doesn't matter."

John: "Goodbye Ian"

"Bye bye."

Hornsby stood up from the defense table and began his cross-examination.

"… when this first happened, you're gathering the facts and trying to figure out not just what happened but why it happened, right?"

"Yes."

"And so, a lot of collateral information would be important to delve into this, right?"

"Yes."

"I guess the first thing is, why not speak to Ian?"

"Well, that was originally the goal. We were supposed to take him back to the police department. I was supposed to interview him. When he got back to the police department, he claimed that he was having a panic attack."

Another detective was already at the hospital with Sue-Ellen, so Horst did not go with Ian to interview him there. He said his supervisor decided not to have anyone interview him until the next day.

"And Ian was in the hospital because of some type of panic attack, right?" Hornsby asked.

"That's correct."

"OK. And talking about John Anselmo, somebody had suggested they thought that John might have a part in this, right?"

"Yes."

Hornsby asked if John seemed "indifferent to the whole situation" at the hospital.

"Yes, he did."

"And did that seem strange to you?

"Yes."

"And so, he basically had this emotional disconnect, right?"

"Yes."

"Okay. And you also spoke to the children, right? Because it's important to get an understanding of what was going on in the household that caused this right?"

"Mhmmm."

"And these children all worship John, right?"

"Yes. Well, they had a lot of respect for him," he answered Hornsby.

"They seem very dedicated to their father, right?"

"Very dedicated, yes,"

"And they had what you, I believe, called a centralized family?"

"Yes."

"And the children also shared John's indifference to the fact that Sue Ellen was on her deathbed, right?

"They didn't have too many emotions regarding her condition."

"Okay. But after she actually passed John's behavior changed dramatically, right?"

"Upon initially telling him that she had passed, yes."

"What did he do? Tell the jury."

"He screamed out, dropped to his knees and beat the ground with his fist"

"Okay. And the way he was sounding, did he sound kind of like the really screaming type thing?"

"Yes, that is correct, sir."

"Just like why did you die, right? Just over the top, right? I mean you can be honest. I mean, I know it looks like a fool doing it. That's what was; it was over the top, right?"

"It was a strong reaction,"

"And that's completely opposite of how he had been acting while she was basically on her deathbed?"

"Yes."

"Okay. But then after she dies, reacts that way, he tries to start giving you evidence of Sue-Ellen's mental health issues, right?"

"That's correct."

"And did that strike you as odd?"

"Yes."

"Because Sue Ellen didn't cause her own death, right? I mean we can be honest, she didn't, right?"

"That's correct."

"And he never really told you why that would be relevant, right?"

"I think he just wanted to, you know, see evidence of her mental state during that time."

"Okay. And speaking of mental state, John did give you, I believe, the text messages that he had been exchanging between himself and Sue-Ellen, right?"

"Yes, he did."

"And he also, I guess it was explained to you at some point, that these text messages, that Ian would basically also send messages indicating they would be, hi, this is Ian, or something like that, right?"

"Yes."

The messages from John accused Sue-Ellen of taking Ian's medicine, Hornsby pointed out.

"And there's nothing in your report indicating that you made any attempts to try to locate the medicine for Ian Ansemo, right?"

"Right."

"And you did know that Ian was not on his medications at the time of the incident, right?"

"I was told that, yes."

"Was that by John?"

"Yes."

"Okay. And just to, I guess, foreclose this possibility between the time the incident happened and basically when you spoke with John Anselmo, he had no ability to talk to Ian, right or, to let's say contrive a defense other than what would have been on through the jail phone calls, right?"

"That's right."

Hornsby then brought up the incident where Rajko threatened to kill Sue-Ellen. Horst said he heard a recording of the incident.

"And did that strike you as odd that a 5-year-old would be screaming that he was going to kill his mother if she wasn't pregnant?"

"Yes."

CHAPTER 19

FROM "MEAT GLOVES" TO PRINCESS

Defense attorney strategy 101 is to get the jury to focus on anyone or anything other than your client. So, when the state tried to exclude evidence of Sue-Ellen's mental state, Judge Welke agreed that she was not on trial. Nor was John.

Hornsby, however, said he needed leeway.

"I believe in this issue and I believe that this jury, unless they get the full Anselmo, won't understand how crazy not only Ian Anselmo became, but all of his family. And I apologize to Sue-Ellen's family for even them having to listen to this stuff. That's how important it is to his defense."[60]

The judge told Hornsby to "keep this reeled in."

Hornsby said he would do his best. "I told Mr. Camuccio about the time I had a meeting with Mr. Anselmo about his testimony and frankly I had my own concerns about, you know, being in the same room."

---

60. Trial transcript, Volume 5, April 10, 2024.

Camuccio later confided, "I thought he [John] was going to come across the table at me."[61]

John, wearing all-black clothing to match his dark beard, climbed onto the witness stand and lowered his face to the microphone to give his full name.

"John Robert George James Jody Anselmo."

"And all these are your, after John and before Anselmo, are all your middle names?"

"Correct."

He said Ian's biological mother stayed with the family until Ian was 6 or 7 and she signed away her parental rights.

He said he met Sue-Ellen in school when he was turning 18.

"It was love at first sight for me and for her. I was completely in love with her from the moment I saw her. I had to meet her parents and I went to church with them. And then after a little while, I realized that she's still in high school, she has her whole life ahead of her. She had just turned 16. And I was a bum. I mean I was a punk rock kid. I was living in a basement. I had nothing going for me at the time. And so, then I decided to break it off. That was the best thing to do."

He said in his deposition that he saw her again nine years later when both were students at the community college. "So I talked to her and I said, 'Listen, you know, I love you and everything else.' And then we spent the night together talking about our future. And I left my wife, I was married at the time. \\

During his testimony at trial, John recalled the day Ian was born. And it was a joyous day. And then soon after that my first wife went berserk and she attacked me."

---

61. Interview with Camuccio for this book.

Prosecutor Weiczorek, knowing where this was headed, objected.

"And Judge, just for the record, I hundred percent agree that how could Ian ever know about this," Hornsby said at the bench conference. "But that's the whole point. That's what Dejah testified to, is that John feeds these kids information and they internalize it as if it's their own experiences."

The judge agreed to give a special instruction to the jury. "…any testimony about other witnesses or events Ian Anselmo did not witness or participate in are not being offered for their truth, but for the effect on the state of mind of Ian Anselmo."

John testified that Ian was born with the umbilical cord wrapped around his neck, that he almost died.

"…obviously he doesn't have a personal memory of that event, right?"

"No."

"But you've told him about that event many times, right?"

"Of course."

He also testified that about a month later his first wife struck his head with a telephone and scratched him. "And I grabbed the baby and I tried to get away from her. Neighbors called the police."

"Okay. But the important thing is you told Ian this whole story, right?"

"Oh yeah."

He said he was in the Army in Texas when Eric was born, and that she left and took the children to Florida.

He told the children that their mother had "kidnapped" them.

"And so, they were fearful that they might be kidnapped again?"

"Yep."

He said his wife was diagnosed with bipolar disorder and trichotillomania "where you rip your hair out," and he told Ian about that, too.

"Okay. And why did you feel it was necessary to tell your child about his mother's mental health issues?"

"Well, I guess that's just who I am."

When it came to the children, he said, "I'm the motherly one." "...I guess I just end up with women who are more of the masculine role. They're more, you know, matter of fact, and I like children, you know. I like playing with kids. I like to coddle the children. I stay up with them at night when they are sick. I'm with them. I mean the whole spiel, you know. It was me."

He said even though Sue-Ellen had "problems" she was not "a bad person." Among the problems initially was smoking marijuana and drinking too much. The children called it "mommy juice," he said.

He said in 2007, she began seeing the family therapist and was diagnosed with attention deficit disorder and given medication.

Hornsby asked what kinds of things the children saw for themselves.

"Screaming, breaking dishes, hanging her head against the walls and on the ground, biting herself, biting me, hitting me...."

He also said she went into his "personal drawer" in the kitchen one day where he kept a handgun and threatened to shoot herself.

He said he stayed with her, "because she was my dream girl."

He said she spent too much on herself, buying expensive clothing and racking up big credit card bills.

He adopted Chloe because Sue-Ellen begged him to.

"...she was a funny-looking little girl and she had big, big, I used to call her Meat Gloves all the time."

"You're talking about her hands, right?"

"She had big, big hands and big wrists. She could do 236 push-ups. She was amazing, okay? She could do all of these physical things. My father said, 'You shouldn't be calling Meat Gloves, you shouldn't be doing that or the other. You should probably call her something pretty and nice.'

"The prettiest girl, besides her own mother in all of literature, because I read these looks, was Dejah-Thoris. And she's the princess of Helium and a Princess of Barsoon, of Mars. So then because she's the ultimate damsel in distress I thought what a fitting name for this little girl who loves me so much because we were very close. And she loved me and I loved her very much."

Edgar Rice Burroughs has his character John Carter describe the princess this way: "Her face was oval and beautiful in the extreme, her every feature was finely chiseled and exquisite, her eyes large and lustrous and her head surmounted by a mass of coal black, waving hair, caught loosely into a strange yet becoming coiffure. Her skin was of a light, reddish copper color, against which the crimson glow of her cheeks and the ruby of her beautifully molded lips shone with a strangely enhancing effect.

"She was destitute of clothes as the green Martians who accompanied her; indeed, save for her highly wrought ornaments she was entirely naked, nor could any apparel have enhanced the beauty of her perfect and symmetrical figure."[62]

Anselmo said she "begged and begged and begged" her mother to have her name changed.

Dejah had a different take on the way John looked at her and said so on Facebook in January 2023.

"When I was little like 9 or 10 my dad took a picture of me sleeping. Made fun of me for years about that picture saying sarcastically how I was 'sleeping beauty' because I was ugly."

One night, she said, Dolan playfully videotaped her sleeping. She was furious. So, I told him that story and why it's not okay, and I'm so insecure when I'm sleeping.

"He said "You are absolutely breathtaking. Not even just pretty. It's literally an honor to be able to look at you" and just like that I married the man healing my traumas."

The questions then turned to cloistering the children.

John said he worked for the Lake County school system from 2007 to 2015.

Before that, the children were allowed to play with neighbor kids, but when he was dismissed from the school system he decided to put up a fence, "…other families started to look at me a certain way."

---

62. Edgar Rice Burroughs, *A Princess of Mars*, 2023, SeaWolf Press.

The children were pulled out of public school and put into virtual school.

"Sue-Ellen thought that was a good decision," he said.

CHAPTER 20

THE 'INSULAR LIFE'

John was consistent in his testimony claiming Sue-Ellen was mentally ill, and it was no surprise that Rajko, "the golden boy," and Nico followed suit.

Asked what role Sue-Ellen played in the home, Nico said, "Sue-Ellen was not a role, just an entity. She caused problems, she was disruptive."[63]

She also described her as "very mentally ill."

Nico repeated the story about Sue-Ellen going into John's "personal drawer" to get a gun and threaten to shoot herself.

"Why did your dad keep a pistol in the kitchen?"

"That's his business not mine. That's his personal drawer."

"In the kitchen?"

"What's that supposed to mean?"

---

63. Frank Stanfield, "Victim's family testifies in trial," *Daily Commercial*, April 14, 2024.

Rajko said Ian was like a "second father." Asked if Sue-Ellen was maternal, he said, "Absolutely not."

On cross-examination, Nico interrupted Camuccio when he said, "When Sue-Ellen didn't come home the day before her murder for...."

"Why do you keep referring to her as that? I mean it's a little harsh. It's my mom, dude."

"Okay. Now it's your mom." Rajko referred to Sue-Ellen by her name seven times.

"Well, yeah, because it is my mom. I just don't refer to her as "mom." There's a difference," Nico said.

Hornsby asked her about the day Ian ran out of the house to meet with Sue-Ellen.

"... is it that unusual for someone in your family to run out of the house?"

"Yes."

"Why? Is it dangerous out there?"

"Why do you say it like that?"

"... did you have an unnatural fear that something was going to happen to you guys?"

"That's foolish."

"Okay, then why didn't you guys ever go outside the house?"

"Because we had no interest to. And besides, Florida is very, very hot."

She finally conceded that it was unusual, "especially with how safety oriented we were, yes."

Among his first questions, Hornsby asked her to tell him the name of her biological mother.

"I do not know. I don't know anything about her and I've never met her."

She said she had no regrets about attacking Dejah in the cemetery.

"Did you try to strangle her?" Hornsby asked.

"I was trying to take out her eyes because she ruined our family. Because of her my mother is dead. Because of her my brother's going away forever."

Nico, who by this time was almost 21, was defiant and annoyed when Hornsby said that she and her siblings lived "a very … insular life."

She acknowledged that she had no adult friends.

"Do you feel like that's strange at all?"

"Not at all."

"Why not?"

"Because I live in a house with the most wonderful people in the whole world, the people that I love, my family. What more could you possibly ask for? I have my father and my six brothers. I wake up every day to … watch [and] grow the minds and the spiritual soul of my younger brothers."

"Okay. But you've never had any curiosity of what's behind your house that you live in?"

"I have no desire whatsoever."

She said she had an email pen pal but declined to say how they met. She said he was a magazine editor.

She said she embraced the Anselmo lifestyle because "this is what I love."

"What is 'this?' Hornsby asked.

"I have chosen to live with my family and to help my father raise the children because my father has a very bad back and he struggles with being able to do things with the children like he used to. So, I have taken up a role to help facilitate the information or teach them throughout the day. So, me and my father go over lesson plans of what the children are supposed to learn and teach them in the mornings and in the afternoon.

Hornsby asked what she would do if something happened to her father.

"My father has given me all the tools I need to help take care of this family if anything should happen to ever happen."

Hornsby got Rajko to talk about Ian's obsession with toys. "We've talked about how Ian's kind of like a child," Hornsby said to Rajko. "Would you say he's a child in a man's body?"

"Absolutely."

"Do you know who Slash and Puppy are?"

"Slash is a toy that he used to carry around or still carries around. And Puppy is a stuffed dog."

"Does he, like, interact with these things as if they're real?"

"He did, yes."

"Okay. How long did that last till?'

"Since he got them. He got Slash in 2014 and he's had Puppy for as long as I can remember.

"…at some point does one stop interacting with these things?"

"Up until this incident he was still interacting with these things. Talking to them. They would talk back to him. He'd feed them. That sort of thing.

"Did that seem abnormal to you?"

"Not at the time, no."

"Does it seem abnormal to you now?"

"Absolutely."

"Did you have a similar toy that you talked to?"

"Yeah. I mean as children do."

"Did you stop at a more normal age, though?

"Yeah."

"What age was that?"

"Ten, eleven."

Rajko also testified about the effect of Ian's medication being disrupted. "We didn't know that he hadn't taken his pills since Friday morning."[64]

That would have been two days after Sue-Ellen left on March 6, which was a Wednesday.

He said Ian became extremely sick. "That was Saturday night after we had that morning driven to Sue-Ellen's work and tried to talk to her in person about Ian's pills …."

"He's normally energetic and happy and jovial and we're always having a good time. I had never seen him like this

64. Trial transcript, Volume VI, April 10, 2024.

before. I've never seen him like that since. I mean he just seemed absolutely despondent, totally detached. Just in his own world."

CHAPTER 21

PSYCHOTIC BREAK

Dr. Hector DeLeon, who had treated Ian from 2012 to 2019, testified that he initially concluded that Ian suffered from attention deficit disorder, impulsiveness and anxiety.

He kept seeing Ian after the murder, however, coming up with different opinions -- a bone of contention for Camuccio. It was also highly suspect in the opinion of the state's mental health expert, Dr. Tania Werner.

"He was very much afraid of something happening to his family," DeLeon said. "And in the background, there was a situation where he was allegedly kidnapped by his biological mother, depriving him of contact with his biological father."[65]

Eventually, he diagnosed him with major depressive disorder, recurrent, mild, with features of lack of motivation, sadness, feeling of inadequacy and decreasing drive. He prescribed Lexapro, an antidepressant, and Vyvanse for ADHD in 2018.

---

65. Trial transcript, Vol. VI, April 10, 2024.

He testified that he was aware of the "nature of his family life," and agreed with Hornsby that it was "stunting" Ian's social development.

He said he briefly got Ian to join a Boy Scout program, but he quit because "some of the policies were not compatible with religious beliefs."

Among the new diagnoses was post-traumatic stress syndrome. Symptoms can include peculiar behavior, paranoid thoughts, hallucinations and angry outbursts.

Hornsby also had him testify about Sue-Ellen's call to his office to try to get a prescription refill while he was out of the office on vacation.

"I didn't know what was going on," he said, but it later became clear to him that Ian was suffering from antidepressant withdrawal syndrome, which led to psychosis.

"...a psychotic break could be delusions, could be hallucinations, and it could be significant strong dissociative episodes," he said. "A dissociative event is like an out-of-body experience where you feel that reality is not continuous."

He also concluded that Ian may have also suffered from a condition known as reactive attachment disorder, "the extreme fear of being separated from his family, these extreme concerns about the well-being of his father and his siblings."

DeLeon also said Ian had symptoms of schizotypal disorder.

"It's mostly related to an unusual type of personality but is also sometimes a prequel... sometimes people develop schizophrenia or schizoaffective disorder."

By now, jurors heard terms that included the word "schizo." They undoubtedly had heard of schizophrenia, the most serious illness where patients lose contact with reality.

Schizoaffective disorder has symptoms of schizophrenia and mood disorders like mania or depression. Schizotypal describes patients perceived to be eccentric.[66]

"If Mr. Anselmo had schizophrenia or schizoaffective disorder you would have diagnosed him with that?" Camuccio asked.

DeLeon agreed.

Psychiatrists depend on self-reporting, Camuccio said. "Since the murder, obviously you're relying on what Ian Anselmo and John Anselmo are telling you about what was going on, correct?"

"Yes."

"… I do tend to trust what they are saying," he said, adding that it is "the nature of the patient-doctor relationship."

Camuccio led the physician through the records, back to October 2018 to point out that his only diagnosis before the murder was for major depressive disorder and ADHD.

DeLeon insisted he also diagnosed him with anxiety disorder, but Camuccio took him back to 2014 and under a heading under anxiety disorders, "it says, quote, no worse."

The doctor said it came under a template, which should have been eliminated, and that only current conditions should have been listed.

Camuccio also noted that there was no mention of hallucinations or Ian talking to toys until 2020.

---

66. www.Webmd.com. "Caregiving for schizophrenia."

Hornsby pointed out in his questioning that there was nothing in the records to indicate that Ian was capable of murder.

"Okay. So clearly, based upon your years of treatment of Ian, there had to be something major that triggered for Ian Anselmo to go from a fairly mild-mannered person to strangling his own stepmother, right?"

"Yes."

"And a psychotic break would be the most likely explanation of that, right?"

"Yes."

CHAPTER 22

"EXTREME VIOLATILITY"

Like all expert witnesses, Daniel Buffington, a clinical pharmacologist and toxicologist, boasts impressive credentials. He has a pharmacy doctorate degree and an MBA, worked with Moffitt Cancer, opened a practice in Tampa and teaches at the University of South Florida.

He would be Hornsby's forensics expert on the effects of sudden medication withdrawal, and how in his opinion, it caused psychosis.

He reviewed Ian's records from family psychiatrist Dr. Hector DeLeon, text messages, law enforcement reports on the day of the murder, and pharmacy records.

He concluded that Ian was suffering from antidepressant withdrawal syndrome (Lexapro), or abrupt withdrawal of Vyvanse for his attention deficit disorder.

He deduced from the text messages between John and Sue-Ellen that Ian had been without his medicine for approximately seven days, since she left the family home on March 6 and the prescription was not refilled until March 13.

He described the withdrawal symptoms as starting off with "flu-like body aches, chills, fever, vacillating body temperatures. They can also include confusion, disorientation, at more advanced levels, it can lead to a depending depression, heightened and debilitating anxiety and paranoia "And they can evolve to extreme psychosis."

He said it can also affect motor skills like those Parkinsons patients endure, and dizziness and vertigo.

He classified Ian's mental status as more "advanced" than "moderate," based on the early age of onset and the "diversity of symptoms." Those symptoms, from the beginning, included "anxiety, distraction, anger, irritability, negative thoughts, decreased appetitive, labile affect. Labile affect is a medical term for someone who is unstable. And typically, we mean emotion So, you can be very flat, very tired, very empathetic, very angry in like a roller coaster formula."

Things were under control as long as he was properly medicated, he said.

Hornsby asked if his medication had been administered "religiously" for a decade leading up to March 9. He said yes, based on his review of DeLeon's records.

"And so, the inference we can make is, is that he and his caregivers would have been unfamiliar with the symptoms of withdrawal or how serious they could get?"

"I would agree...."

He said there were also withdrawal symptoms for Vyvanse.

Drugs affect our serotonin... we call them neurotransmitters. Chemicals that our brain naturally produces, and we depend on for clarity of thought, stability, cognitive status, control of emotions and anger."

Hornsby interrupted saying, "and to be clear, all of us in this courtroom today, we have serotonin that's regulating our mental state, correct?"

Buffington agreed and said the drugs also affect two other critical neurotransmitters, epinephrine and dopamine.

Normally, you would gradually decrease medication. Abrupt disruption could result in neuropathies, "where the nerves in the body ... are behaving incorrectly and sending false signals. You can have a change in irritability, change in mood, emotional status, confusion, decreased orientation... you could also have a change in sleep. All of these collectively creating a risk for psychoses.

"Not every patient who has this has psychosis. That would be an extreme scenario."

He defined psychosis as "where you're detached from your surroundings your ability to interpret your surroundings."

There are triggers, he said. And age makes a difference because younger people may not have developed sufficient coping skills.

"We do see an emergence of mental health disorders in teens and twenties. But this is a case where it was even preceding teens. This was at adolescence and already having to be on advanced medication therapy to control it. The polar withhold of that therapy would be even more magnitude at this stage."

Buffington, who created an elaborate chart to explain symptoms, also explained that withdrawal affects both cognitive thought and mood. "... we all have and depend on the neurotransmitters to be in a good place."

He said he is a believer in not just medication, but talk therapy and analyzing other factors, including nature vs. nurture.

He used the analogy of a pebble thrown into a lake. When everything is going well, the water is calm. A pebble causes ripples. "And it's also what happens when you start a medication."

Finally, after leading Buffington through his extensive testimony, Hornsby got to a key part of the expert's opinion.

He referred to part of DeLeon's report that says that a person undergoing a traumatic event might have a "depersonalization or detachment from reality," and they may not recall it.

"The lack of memory of memory of specific events or specific time periods actually is consistent with psychosis," Buffington said.

He said that it was his opinion that the "totality" of the effects of drug withdrawals resulted in psychosis.

It was a severe case, he said.

Hornsby said, "And in Ian's case, those extreme aggravators, I guess we'll call them... [are] the chaotic or the family life he had going on, right?"

"That is an understatement."

"... as someone's taken off their medications, and if they're frequently having, let's say, signs of hope and then signs of despair within short periods of time, can that further exacerbate how they're going to react or suffer from the withdrawal syndrome?"

Buffington said the threat to strangle Sue-Ellen with her intestines was "extreme psychotic behavior."

And that was followed by him begging and pleading and telling her that he loves her and wants to be with her. "And expressing sympathy for the other kids in the house and trying to return to a sense of stability and normality."

Hornsby, referring to it Buffington's analogy of a pebble causing a ripple effect on water, said it seemed more like a boulder causing big waves "right up to when he got in the car with Sue-Ellen Anselmo."

"Correct, that's an excellent analogy."

Wieczorek, on cross-examination, brought out the fact that Buffington did not interview any witnesses, that he never spoke to Ian, and that the only deposition he read about Ian's life was John's. Nor did he view any bodycam video.

"And so, you based your opinion, at least in part, upon a review of John Anselmo, Ian's father's statement having to assume that he would be a truthful or reliable historian?"

"And Sue-Ellen's statements as well."

"And by Sue-Ellen's statements you're referring to those text messages?'

"Correct."

"And so, you based your opinion on a belief that Ian's stepmother took Ian's medications with her when she left the house on March the 6th?"

"Correct. And that both parents were acknowledging he was without them."

Hornsby, knowing that John's credibility was in question, pointed to a text message between him and Sue-Ellen.

"On March 9 at 10:47 p.m., does John Anselmo tell Sue-Ellen Anselmo, 'Please tell me where Ian's medicine is.

He is having a horrible time. Stop being selfish and write back?'"

Buffington acknowledged that is what the text said.

Sue-Ellen texts back: "I don't know where it is. Which one? I will take care of it ASAP."

John responds with one word: Vyvanse. "And then he does follow up with, 'I asked you a couple of days ago. If he gets any worse, I am taking him to the hospital You are destroying the family."

Buffington responded by saying there were "multiple days" of discussions about this prior to the 9th.

Hornsby said, "...assuming that John is fabricating all of this, he would have had to have really planned out laying the foundation for this antidepressant withdrawal defense that I'm presenting five years later, three days before her death, right?"

"Yeah. But I don't see the secondary strategy happening. He's simply asking for ...."

"Right. That's the point."

"Yes."

"The point is that, sure, John probably isn't a reliable reporter in general, but we know he's being truthful with this because he's reporting in real time to Sue-Ellen that it's so bad that I'm thinking of taking the kid to the hospital."

CHAPTER 23

"VIRUS OF THE MIND"

Defense psychologist William Steven Saunders, Ph.D., worked for the Federal Bureau of prisons for seven years before starting his own practice in 2005. The forensic psychologist said he also taught at the University of Central Florida.

Much of his work is court-appointed to see if defendants are mentally competent to stand trial, which would seem to make him uniquely qualified for the trial.

He interviewed Ian four years earlier, administered tests, reviewed jail records, Dr. DeLeon's reports, and court records.

Asked how long he spoke with Ian, he said: "It was quite a while. He was very emotional on that day. It was difficult to get through that interview. We stopped and started several times. I think … he was probably in the office three or four hours."[67]

---

67. Trial transcript, Vol. VIII, April 11, 2024.

Of the tests, some were self-reporting, and one test checked for malingering, or faking, which he passed, according to Saunders. One test was designed to see if Ian was autistic. It was filled out by John.

"There were some indications from the medical records that Ian may have a psychotic disorder such as schizophrenia."

As a child and a teenager, he was treated for depression, anger control, frustration, and anxiety. "A lot of mood disturbances," he said.

Hornsby asked him to give his own opinion. "I diagnosed him with major depressive disorder, recurrent moderate with psychotic features. Basically, sometimes a person's mood disorder can become so great that they detach from reality, and I believed that Ian was suffering from a psychotic disorder.

"I diagnosed him with attention deficit hyperactivity disorder," he said, explaining that it was a pre-existing condition.

He concluded that he also had autism spectrum disorder and reactive attachment disorder.

"Basically, I think a big part of what was going on with Ian, as well as developmentally, is that he had a lot of disruptive attachments in his early life and this caused this sense of not being able to properly bond with the parental figures."

"Would this, for example be his internalized belief that his biological mother kidnapped him and then subsequently abandoned him?"

"I wouldn't think that those two things are necessarily linked. I think that's more of a psychotic delusional belief. But certainly, the reactive detachment disorder contributed to that."

He said he also diagnosed him with post-traumatic stress disorder.

"I didn't rule out a schizoaffective disorder. Often schizoaffective disorder is basically schizophrenia plus a mood disorder. And depending on how those things are presenting, if the psychosis part is more predominant, then often a person may get diagnosed with schizoaffective. If the mood part is more predominant, then usually a mood disorder is given.

On the day I saw him, it seemed that his mood disorder and anxiety were far more prevalent than the psychotic part, although I do believe the psychotic part was a component of that, and that's why I diagnosed him the way I did."

"Now, when he saw you, he was compliant with his medication, correct?"

"Yes, I believe so."

"And so, when you're compliant with your medication, are these symptoms, I'll use psychotic symptoms, are they obviously going to be suppressed if you're properly taking your medication?"

"Yes, that's the hope."

Hornsby kept pressing.

"...in terms of pure safety, we can't take away a mentally ill person's medication to determine whether or not they, in fact, have these psychotic underlying issues, correct?"

"I think that would be an unethical kind of experimentation. I mean, no, you wouldn't want to do that."

"Right. And that's exactly the point. Even while medicated you believe that there was a suggestion that he had these underlying issues, correct?"

"Yes."

Hornsby then had him check the boxes, so to speak, that he was mentally ill at the time of the offense.

"Is it your opinion that, based upon this condition, that at the time of the offense when Mr. Anselmo strangled his stepmother, he did not know what he was doing?"

"That's what I believe, yes."

He said he based his opinion of Ian having a psychotic break based on the "exhaustive records," videos, arrest records and his interview with Ian.

He agreed with Hornsby that the wild mood swings in the text messages were the sign of a break.

He also agreed that the sudden withdrawal of his antidepressant medication could possibly lead to a psychotic episode.

"That's a test of basically a person's functioning, you know, having the ability to get along in the world, relate to things. Ian was definitely delayed from where he should be when compared to his same aged peers."

He did not have the skills to live on his own, Saunders said.

"Okay. In terms of individuals knowing what's right and wrong, does the age matter? Meaning, does a younger child, their understanding of right and wrong gonna be the same level as an adult about, you know, conducting themselves appropriately within society?"

"No, it isn't."

"Okay. And if Ian's developmental age is severely stunted, would his ability to realize that his reactions to social exposures were inappropriate or right or wrong relative to his actual biological age?"

"It would have made a determination more difficult, certainly."

Hornsby asked when symptoms of schizophrenia typically show up. Saunders explained that it was usually in the teens or early adulthood.

"And that's where Ian biologically fell at the time of this incident?"

"Yes."

Saunders said he saw symptoms of it but not enough to make a diagnostic opinion.

He defined major depressive disorder as "in many ways a disturbance of consciousness. It is a sense of detachment from the self. You don't feel really kind of who you are. That's why when you move to the extreme ends of those kinds of disorders you can develop possible psychotic symptoms. And that psychosis that detaches from reality can be very much linked to a mood disorder. But even people with schizophrenia, you know, will manifest mood kinds of symptoms as well. So, I mean it's not to be downplayed at all. It's a very serious illness."

One of the issues of diagnosing him the day he saw Ian, he said, was that he was on medication, "so he wasn't really manifesting a lot of psychosis. I mean, mostly it was emotional volatility with him on that day. He was very distraught and difficult to get answers out of."

Hornsby asked if talking to toys at his age could be a sign of underlying psychosis. "It could," he said.

Camuccio began had begun his cross-examination by asking: "… is it fair to say that the strongest area of evidence supporting your overall opinion is the defendant saying he does not remember the act itself?"

"I don't know if that's the strongest. It certainly is, you know, one of the criteria that I look at."

"…let's say everything about this case is the same; his prior history, what was going on at the house, everything, but when it came down to it, he said, 'I was angry with my stepmom, I went over there, I strangled her, I remember doing it, I wrapped that cord around her neck and I killed her,' we wouldn't be having this conversation here today, correct?"

"Oh, this is a hypothetical?"

"Yes."

Camuccio continued: "If he were to say that and he were to say, 'I remember the event, I did it, I meant to do it, no matter what was going on in the home beforehand, you would agree that insanity would not be appropriate?"

"Probably not. I mean that's a broad-based hypothetical, so you'd have to look at all the other factors. But that certainly would be a big nail in the coffin."

"If he said, this is why I did something, you would agree with me that would be evidence that he was sane at the time of the offense?"

"Not necessarily." He said he would consider it, however.

Camuccio pointed out several specific, cogent things that Ian said to the police at the cemetery.

"…at the scene, Ian Anselmo is clearly saying, 'My dad is gonna be so pissed, correct?'"

"That's right."

"All right. That is an indication that he knows what he did was wrong at that moment, correct?"

"I don't know if you can say that. You know, I'm not 100 percent certain what was going through his mind at that moment. You can interpret that in a logical way to say it."

"Okay. So, getting to that point of we don't really know what's going on in his mind, you would agree with me that a lot of what we have to do is rely on his report and the reports of John Anselmo about what was going on, correct?"

"Those are factors that you would have to look at, correct."

"And you agree with me that they have an interest in this case?"

"Certainly."

"And when Ian Anselmo says, I don't know what happened when the actual homicide was occurring, there are explanations for that other than mental health, correct?" He could be lying, Camuccio pointed out, or experiencing a moment of amnesia.

He then switched to DeLeon's records. "You would agree with me that there is not a single mention in here whatsoever of him talking to toys, stuffed animals or anything like that?"

He agreed.

Saunders also agreed that he could not rule out schizoaffective disorder when he met with Ian in 2020. Camuccio pointed out that Ian continued seeing DeLeon after the murders. SSaS

"At this stage, Ian is 26 years old and he still has not diagnosed him either schizophrenia or schizoaffective disorder."

"Okay."

"So, with that, at this point, we'll rule those out."

"I haven't seen Ian since 2020, so you would have to ask Dr. Deleon about that."

"Okay. He did diagnose him with schizotypal, but he did not diagnose him specifically with any schizophrenia or schizoaffective disorder."

"Okay."

Switching gears, Camuccio asked what pieces of evidence he had reviewed. He had looked at arrest bodycam video, but not footage when he was placed in an ambulance, or when he arrived at the hospital for his anxiety attack, or his jail calls.

Camuccio then brought up what would turn out to be a key bone of contention. "There is not a single notation that references what the defendant told you about that?"

"That's right."

"And that's because you didn't ask him about what happened that day; you relied on all these other sources, correct?"

"I attempted to ask him about what happened that day. But as I had stated earlier, he was so emotionally distraught, it was difficult to get a lot out of him."

Yet, that was the thing he was hired to find out, Camuccio pointed out.

Saunders' report said Ian had been without his Lexapro for five to seven days. He said he got that from a note in DeLeon's report. He said he "does not recall" if he discussed that with Ian. It was not in his report.

As for the bodycam video, he agreed that Ian corrected an officer about the spelling of his name, how his father would be angry, about making sure officers did not overlook his rosary, and giving details to the 911 operator.

"During the 911 call he tells the 911 operator he remembers having an argument, right?"

"Correct."

"You admit in the 911 call and the body camera footage the defendant is clearly upset and distraught?"

"Yes."

"And once again though, you would agree that that behavior very well could be consistent with an individual with absolutely no mental health issues that was in a situation handcuffed after just committing a murder? You would agree that a person without any sort of mental health condition could exhibit that same behavior?"

"I mean, that's the same hypothetical posed earlier that I agreed to, so yes."

"Okay. During that seven years' worth of prior psychiatric history that we have documented with Dr. DeLeon, the only two diagnoses was ADHD and the major depressive, mild…."

Saunders conceded that the ADHD probably did not play a role in the murders.

Camuccio showed him a copy of his deposition.

"And you agree that autism by itself would not have contributed in this case?"

"I don't think any of the illnesses by themselves would have contributed necessarily."

As for PTSD, Saunders agreed with Camuccio when he said, "when you are diagnosing somebody with PTSD, you have to take them as you see them at that point."

"And at the time you did that diagnosis, the defendant had been charged with the murder of his stepmother?"

"Yes."

"You would agree with me that that is a traumatic event which symptoms of PTSD at the time you saw him could be based on?" Camuccio asked.

He agreed that this could be the case.

"Prior to the murder, he had never been diagnosed with PTSD, correct?"

"As far as I know."

"So, the symptoms and diagnosis that you came to and concluded very well could be from the traumatic event that led to his arrest, as opposed to anything prior to the arrest. Would you agree with that?"

"No."

"Okay. You stated that the defendant's belief that he had been kidnapped by his biological mother, I think you referred to that as a psychotic delusional belief. Is that what you said?"

"Yes."

"Okay, and that's some belief that's reflected in the records with Dr. Deleon?"

"That's right."

"Now, if the fact that he was, quote, kidnapped by his biological mother and driven over state lines is exactly what his father has been telling him his entire life, that's the only belief he would have about that event, correct?"

"I mean that's part of how we frame our view of reality is what others tell us, yes."

"So, if that's the basis of this information, that's not a psychotic belief, that's just him being groomed based on what his father told him. Is that fair?"

"Well, it's a belief not based on reality."

"But if it's the only thing he has ever been told is just not true, that's not psychosis, that's just, you're relying on information that's not true, correct?"

"It would depend on the basis of that statement and why the father gave those statements."

"If I was told from a young age that Florida was the 50th state to join the union, and I just went on about my life and that's the only thing I had ever been told, and I had no ability to draw or figure out anything else, and I said, 'Florida was the 50th state in the union,' would that mean I'm psychotic because I'm relying on information that was given to me that's just not true?"

"No. That's just a factual error. It wouldn't cause a disturbance in your reality… I mean, it wouldn't be a traumatic event, in other words."

"Correct. No further questions, judge."

Hornsby, on redirect, attacked the hypotheticals that Camuccio had presented.

The first was whether someone could be lying.

"That's always gonna be a possibility no matter what situation we're in?"

"That's right."

The second hypothetical, Saunders said, "was a person could have a lapse in memory and not be mentally ill, and certainly that can be the case. But I don't think it's the case in this case. Right. Because it's undisputed that Ian Anselmo, prior to March 6, 2019, suffered from a mental illness, right?

"Yes, that's undisputed."

So, that met the first "prong," he said, of the legal definition of insanity.

"Okay. And so, at the end of the day, the only thing that never really would be disputed is whether or not, because of that event, that the mental illness on the day in question when he committed the act, that he did not know what he was doing was wrong, right?"

"That's right."

"And if I'm correct, bringing that home, is that you're saying that due to the crisis and events that he was going through, the withdrawal of the medication … he had a psychotic break during his interactions with Sue Ellen?"

"I think it's clear that he did."

"Okay. Because normal, happy people don't have psychotic breaks out of nowhere, right?"

"Typically, not."

Hornsby said it was obvious that there was some type of "triggering mechanism" in his interaction with Sue-Ellen that caused a psychotic break.

Saunders agreed, though he said some people develop psychosis gradually.

Hornsby pointed to the 911 call. "And immediately after the event, he's being asked a specific question; did he strangle his mother, "and he's saying I don't know."

Saunders said psychosis shows up in different ways, including moments of lucidity. "…you can sit down and have a conversation that seems, on its face, rather coherent, and then they just go off on a tangent and you realize you're dealing with someone who is completely divorced from reality."

Hornsby brought up the PTSD diagnosis and Ian's belief, through John, that he had been kidnapped by his biological mother.

"Is it fair to say that his father appeared to be infecting with a virus of the mind regarding all these delusional beliefs …?"

"I definitely think it's the toxic family system, without a doubt. And I think that his father did infect him quite a bit with a lot of ideas that weren't necessarily based on reality, that contributed to both trauma and … his eventual psychotic break."

"Is that type of influence by, especially a father figure, is that dangerous to a mentally ill person?"

"It's very dangerous."

Switching topics, Hornsby asked him to define a cult.

"…typically a group of individuals that are ruled over by typically a single individual and similar in nature, the cult members are not allowed to reach out beyond cult members for support or for information. Their information is typically limited. There's a high degree of control the cult leader has over different members. And they're not allowed to have any kind of really independent thought is the ultimate aim of most cults."

Cults are harmful, Saunders said. People need a "safe place" to relax after a stressful event, and if you don't have one it will wear you down.

Camuccio got in one more shot in his rebuttal.

"…at the time that I deposed you, I sked you about all of your opinions as it relates to this case and the mental health of the defendant, correct?"

"Correct."

"And at no time did you bring up the fact that you thought that anything about cult behavior or father influence had any effect on what happened on March 13, 2019, correct?"

"That's right.

CHAPTER 24

REALITY OF BLOODY HANDS

The state's psychiatrist witness, Dr. Tania Werner, is the chief medical officer and vice president of a community health center in Gainesville. "I also manage an inpatient unit, a psychiatric unit and then I do forensic psychiatry," she said.[68]

She reviewed medical records, the defense expert's reports, bodycam video from the scene, the hospital, and the ambulance. She also reviewed deposition transcripts from John Anselmo and other family members.

Most importantly, she interviewed Ian for two hours in 2022. His defense team was present.

She described the process as starting off with general questions about their family, education, work and medical history. Psychiatric issues. Any substance issues. And legal issues. Have they ever been arrested before? Been in trouble?"

---

68. Trial transcript, Vol. VIII, April 11, 2024.

The next stage is what she called a mental status examination, "a series of questions that you ask to understand their orientation. Do they know who they are, where they are, why they're there, what's going on. It tests their education level. You know, are they normal, below average or above average?"

One of the questions is about the current president, and how far back can the person go in naming his predecessors.

"He named the current president and nine of his predecessors."

There are also questions to test abstract thought, such as the similarities between two objects and simple calculations.

The next stage was designed to test his sanity. She said she generally starts a day or two before the incident and then asks questions about what happened at the time.

She said she diagnosed Ian with major depressive disorder, generalized anxiety disorder, and with a history of attention deficit hyperactivity disorder.

Camuccio brought up Dr. DeLeon's diagnoses.

"… as you went through those records, were you able to observe the fact that the same treating physician gave him more diagnoses after the homicide than had previously been diagnosed before the homicide?"

"Correct. I believe that was changed after the second time he met with him following the murder."

He asked if she saw any reference to psychosis in the previous seven years.

"Absolutely not."

"And did you see any evidence of any sort of hallucinations?"

"No."

"Delusions?"

"No."

"Now, post-homicide, the records in (DeLeon's) Advanced Behavioral Services indicate some discussion of Ian talking to his toys."

"Yes."

"And was there any discussion of that in any of the records prior?"

"No."

She said she disagreed with DeLeon's diagnosis of schizotypal, the personality disorder with odd behavior and odd thoughts, because he did not meet the required five out of nine criteria.

She also disagreed with the PTSD diagnosis. "…if he didn't have post-traumatic stress disorder prior to the homicide, you can't relate his behaviors or activities at the time of the homicide to that diagnosis."

Nor did she diagnose him with autism or reactive attachment disorder. "Even if he met the criteria for those two diagnoses, none of the symptoms attributable for those two diagnoses would account for him not knowing his actions or the consequences…."

Camuccio pointed out that Saunders ruled out schizoaffective disorder and noted that she did not diagnose Ian with schizophrenia.

Schizophrenia typically shows up in teens or early 20s, she said, noting that he was 26 at trial.

The prosecutor went back to Saunders saying the family was like a cult.

It would be "influential," she conceded. "But it would not … make it so that he did not understand or appreciate what he was doing or the consequences of his actions."

Camuccio asked her if Ian had lived "a sheltered life."

"Yes, absolutely."

"Does that mean he is insane?

"No."

He then asked, "Does psychosis automatically mean insane?"

"… people can have auditory hallucinations or visual hallucinations that are totally unrelated to whatever criminal activity they have. So, the two do not equally jive."

He was sane at the time of the crime, she said, and the 911 call, bodycam footage showed that he knew what had happened was wrong. There was another factor, she said, "a lot of anger" evidenced by his threat to strangle her with her own intestines and his jail call to John saying Sue-Ellen had "ruined the family."

During cross-examination, she agreed with Hornsby that Ian "lived in a cult-like atmosphere," and that the children were "enmeshed within the father."

She explained it this way in her deposition: "I think it was a very enmeshed relationship with her and with the dad. And he used a lot of 'we' when talking about it, almost like he was the one in the relationship, and our children as opposed to, you know, their children, or my brothers and sisters. It was our children."[69]

She also agreed that Ian's "worldview," as Hornsby put it, came from information presented by John, including the kidnapping story and being born with the umbilical cord wrapped around his neck.

She disagreed with the idea that he was suffering from "some type of hallucinatory or delusional problems" when talking to his toys. "It seemed to be more related to his restrictive upbringing and immaturity."

She also agreed that discontinuation of medications can have side effects, including fidgeting, being irritable and feeling hopeless, but not hallucinations.

Nor did she agree that he suffered from attachment disorder, which she defined as parental neglect.

"Did it appear to you that Ian had been brainwashed by his father?"

"I think there's a certain aspect of that. When he talked about family members that had left kind of the fold of the family, that they weren't compliant, they weren't going along with the family's beliefs or what they were, kind of the basis of their family unit, so they were pushed aside. And then there was no further contact with them, which is very much what you see in cults."

Ian was not insane at the time of the crime, she said.

"And that belief is based upon the fact, that I understand it, is that afterward he was able to determine that he had strangled her by looking at his hands, right?"

"Correct."

69. Deposition of Dr. Werner, March 3, 2023.

Hornsby was referring to her psych eval with Ian, which read: "... Ian Anselmo said after they drove to the cemetery he remembers begging Sue-Ellen not to do this to the children and she responded, "They'll get over it" after which he blacked out and called the police using Sue-Ellen's phone and remained in the backseat crying with his hands covered in blood."

"And he was able to able to recognize that what he had done was wrong... and call 911?"

"Correct."

"And the fact that he was worried about his father being mad at him, right?"

Defense attorney Roseanne Eckert had asked Werner a simple question during her deposition: "...what led up to his meeting her and the strangling?"

"He was angry."

"Okay. Why was he angry?"

"He was angry that she told him that she was not returning to the home and wasn't bringing the children back."

"Okay. And then what happened?"

"He strangled her."

"Okay. And why?"

"Because he was angry."

"And you don't think he remembered that?"

"I'm not sure if he remembers it or not. And I describe that in two ways: Either he remembers it and he's not acknowledging that, versus did he have a dissociative amnesia not wanting to look back, and it's because of the way that memories are stored during a traumatic event."

She compared it to people not remembering the moment of an automobile accident.

"Okay. So, if he did not remember actually strangling her, and wakes up with blood all over his hands, and sees her dead, he would understand that that was wrong after he sees that right?"

"Yes."

"But that does not necessarily mean that if he was in a psychotic state, that he knew what he was doing was wrong and was unable to stop it?"

"But psychosis doesn't come and go like that. It doesn't come and go in two minutes."

He was able to tell the 911 operator where he was and that he had killed his stepmother. "… he knew it was wrong,"

CHAPTER 25

"CRAZY"

Hornsby began his closing argument in one of the most audacious, theatrical performances in the long, bloody history of Lake County crime courtroom battles.

He pulled up a little child's table in front of the jury box, putting Puppy on one chair and Slash on the other, and sat down to begin a conversation with the toys.

"Who am I?" he asked. "My name's Richard. Where are we at? We're in the courtroom right now. What happened? Well, Ian did a bad thing. Yeah, yeah. Ian, while it's no excuse, but John finally got to him. He got to everybody.

"Yeah, that is Chloe behind me. She's the only one that escaped. And she told us that even after she escaped it still took her several years, even after her mother was dead, to be able to escape John's influence. But even now she still considers him her dad, even though she believes that Ian killed her mother, John's the reason that Sue-Ellen's dead.

"So, what happens now? Well, we've heard a lot of people you've probably been listening to. You know, Mr. Camuccio gave a compelling case. And I don't blame him. And now

I have to prove that, convince, eight people... that Ian was insane.

"You know, just talking to you over the years, that doesn't necessarily mean he's insane. Why am I talking to you? Well, I'm exhausted. A week in this courtroom. Emotionally drained. Listening to Chloe having to explain how these kids were beat on a routine basis, how they weren't allowed to have friends, how they were forced to stay inside, how if they showed any disobedience or any lack of absolute subservience, they were beat like dogs. That was exhausting, to have to hear this man was so maniacal. Yeah, I know, I understand that's why Ian probably talked to you because he had nobody.

"Sometimes you can't just put your hands over your ears like he's been doing all week and just hope everything will be okay."

Camuccio broke the spell briefly. "Your honor, objection to references that the defendant…. "

"Mr. Hornsby, he did not testify," Judge Welke admonished.

"Yeah. Yeah. It's exhausting listening to John Anselmo," Hornsby continued. "Yeah, he testified. It was crazy. Crazier than me sitting here right now talking to you."

The only thing crazier, he said, was the testimony of the children. "And I suspect that if any of the other ones walked in after them, it would be just crazy talk."

"Crazy" would be the theme, and he sometimes shouted the word.

He said he brought in "some pretty smart people" like Dr. DeLeon.

"He said, 'I've been treating him for a while and he had these crazy beliefs from, you know, Ian's biological mother and how Ian thinks that she tried to kill him.'"

He said Buffington testified how withdrawal from his medication might cause a psychotic break, and that Dr. Saunders was positive that Ian had a break.

Much of the state's evidence corroborated his, he said.

Hornsby then talked about a harmful contradiction in the evidence. Jurors watched an officer's bodycam video showing Ian saying he had been without his Zoloft for two or three days.

"Yeah, that's not quite what John said in the text messages. But, you know, Dr. Buffington said sometimes the person that's having a crisis event isn't the best person to listen to, that type of information is not the most accurate.

"And so why am I sitting here talking to you instead of talking to the jury? Well, sometimes the only way you can escape is just to bury yourself in your imagination. Ian was basically imprisoned in the Anselmo household. So were the other kids. That's what he did.

"He was able to go on a daily basis, burying himself when he was playing with the siblings, talking to you guys until John wouldn't let him anymore.

"What am I going to do? You guys, I'm going to have to put you back in the back. Turn around to these eight people and convince them that Ian was so insane on March 13, of 2019 that he strangled his stepmother. And it's scary because Mr. Camuccio is right, that's wow, you look at those jury instructions and it's like, what do we even do?

"Well, we do the same thing that Ian's done, Chloe's done and every single one of those Anselmo children said, you keep fighting. You fight through the craziness. Every day's a battle with John Anselmo who's constantly, constantly, constantly bearing down on you. The overbearing narcissistic.

"He drives you insane listening to him on the stand saying the stupidest things that everybody knows is just crazy. Everybody knows that Sue-Ellen's not banging her head against the wall. But if you say it enough you believe, even though you didn't see it.

"If you say it enough you believe your sister is this terrible person because John says it over and over every single day. And it keeps on going. And you bottle it up every single day and you take your meds and you just keep on going. Because every day's a battle unless you can escape that man.

"So, yeah, I'm gonna put you back and I'm gonna take a deep breath. We're gonna convince this jury that Ian did a bad thing but the law excuses him. He's not guilty by reason of insanity. And if you find him not guilty by reason of insanity that's not necessarily the end of it for him, though.

"The judge can commit Ian if he needs treatment. Possibly get him away from John. Get him outpatient treatment. Or maybe if he's allowed, he'll go back to you guys one day. And if he does, I hope he gets the strength that his sister did and escapes that house. I know he's got to."

"WRONG ARGUMENT"

Turning to the jury, he said Sue-Ellen did not deserve to die. Then, acknowledging that "this is the wrong argument to make," said Ian was as much a victim, even though he was still alive.

"And I want to argue to you that John Anselmo killed Sue Ellen, but he did not. And please, Mr. Camuccio is gonna get up here and probably say it, but he's right, that is not the argument. And that's not a reason to find Ian not guilty."

He said Dejah's testimony, while she testified for the state, "corroborated the veracity of everything you heard from my witnesses."

He said he didn't even expect it.

"The crazy man came up here and everything she said that basically he did, except molest her, he said he did. That's crazy. He said he wakes her up in the middle of the night to work out until she's exhausted. She likes to work out. How crazy is that? These are children.

"He says that Rajko was the golden boy and would sleep next to him all the time, until this day. That's crazy. He said that he brainwashed all these children…."

Hornsby said the children were trapped in the house, like prison. "And they have John constantly telling them, 'Sue-Ellen, she does this. She cheats on me. She does drugs. She's unfaithful. She ran away. She can't be trusted, she can't cut men's hair.' And then over and over and over and over and over again. Constantly."

Dejah, in her sworn testimony, said she would not have the fortitude to go back to the house because if she saw Korak she would want to stay.

He reminded them that Dejah said she was trained to only remember the good times. "That's crazy!"

He predicted that Camuccio might say the household seemed crazy but it does not mean Ian was insane. "And he's right." However, the crime occurred in an explosion of emotions when Sue-Ellen left and Ian was without his medicine.

He said Dejah's testimony was one of the saddest he has ever heard. "It was like seeing someone who had been rescued from a cult."

He also alluded to Dejah's cellphone video when Rajko told his father that he would kill Sue-Ellen but she was pregnant.

Again, predicting what Camuccio would say, he said the prosecutor would argue that Rajko knew right from wrong, so he would have been convicted, too.

Hornsby criticized Werner's statement that she would need more information to determine if that was insanity.

"What information do you need? What if I told you that this kid, the 10-year-old, had the same exact upbringing as that kid? But that the 10-year-old has not been diagnosed with a mental illness. What if I told you that, Doc? Well, no, need more information. Okay.

"What if I told you that 30 seconds later, he went there and wrapped it [a blanket around her neck]? Nope, need more information. Okay. But I mean would you crawl inside his head? What are you gonna sit down and tell me? Okay. What's he gonna tell you if he doesn't remember exactly what happened at the event?"

The basis for Dr. Werner's opinion was that a psychotic break takes longer than a couple of minutes.

"But where is the evidence of that? It was never established exactly what time Sue Ellen picked up Ian. Never."

They must have had a conversation. "Did he sit there for 15 minutes before he came to and go, 'Oh my God! I don't know what happened. I think I strangled her.'

"Did you, or you think? 'I think it was an accident.' That's the first thing he said is 'it's an accident.'

"And here's the problem with that. Mr. Hornsby, why are you screaming at us like an idiot? Well, here's the problem. His expert is the only one who testifies to this. She said my opinion could change tomorrow. So, what she's telling you is that after you guys go back there, after listening to five days of this crazy talk, we could find out that he was in that car for 15 minutes before he came to…."

"Wow, you're going to convict somebody based on that opinion? Whoo! That's crazy, too! Let's all be crazy!"

Proving insanity is difficult, he conceded. "…nobody could ever prove sanity. It's always a basic opinion. That's the only way you get it is opinions."

Different experts have different opinions, he noted, but the evidence comes from Dr. DeLeon. "There's nothing to indicate, you know, that he would change his opinion."

DeLeon, in his revised report, included a diagnosis of early signs of schizotypal. Hornsby said Werner found signs of the disorder but not enough to meet the criteria, so she did not include it in her diagnosis.

He also addressed the fact that Ian had been on medications since he was a child, and he talked about the issue of the missing medication, pointing to a text on March 9, 2019.

"So, we have to kind of assume that … Ian's missing his pills is true. Whether or not Sue-Ellen took the pills, I don't know. I wouldn't put it past John to have taken the pills so that he could get his kids all worked up and use them as some type of crutch to blackmail Sue-Ellen into coming back. I don't know. It doesn't even matter."

It is also true that Ian became so physically ill on that Saturday night that he passed out. Ian later told the paramedics that he lost 10 pounds that week.

Hornsby also lashed out at the prosecution, claiming they were accusing him of fabricating the issue of Ian talking to the toys.

Dejah testified to it, he said.

"And then I brought out these pictures, I mean look at this. This is crazy. 2015. Congratulations Ian and Slash. They made a banner for him and his imaginary friend. That's not healthy. Like, he would have been 16 when that would have been made."

The point is, he said, is that Ian is unstable and has been his entire life. "…it's probably partly nature/nurture. Part genetic. Because clearly, they all have mental illnesses. All of them."

He said their "world view" was a dark classroom and a backyard "where they let the landscaping overgrow so they can go on adventures and look at bugs."

He reminded jurors about a deputy testifying that shutters on the home were bizarre. "Why were they bizarre? Obviously, the difference is it's like a compound that he's built. It's like David Koresh or something crazy."

He took jurors through all of the text messages.

"So, in real-time before Sue-Ellen's passing, he's accusing her of all these crazy things that he told you she did. It's called gaslighting, people."

Among the threats to air her dirty laundry was tax fraud and her mental illness.

"And do you want to know what the tax fraud is? It's even crazier. He accuses her, his wife, who is he married to, of illegally taking a tax deduction for one of their own children. It's the stupidest thing you've ever heard. And it's always stupid … for reasonable people, but he convinced these people that this was a real issue in their life."

Hornsby said there were four components that proved Ian's insanity: There was a history of mental illness, he was on managed medication for "his entire life," and that he was "essentially a child in a man's body," and "like autistic."

He finished by saying, "We want justice for Sue-Ellen. I think justice is Ian Anselmo is to be found not guilty by reason of insanity. I think that you shouldn't stop there. Write it. Well, what do you mean, Mr. Hornsby? You've got pen and paper. Write under that verdict of not guilty by reason of insanity, write John Anselmo's guilty. We all know that's the right thing."

CHAPTER 26

CRAZY IS NOT INSANITY

Camuccio immediately attacked Hornsby's arguments in his rebuttal.

"…he got up there and pounded his fists and said very loudly, 'crazy, crazy, crazy, crazy, crazy' because he can't argue from the actual jury instruction about insanity."

Hornsby objected, spurring one of the many, many bench conferences in the trial. He said he specifically mentioned the defense burden of proving clear and convincing evidence.

"I'm just making a point, Judge," Camuccio said. He then turned to the jurors and said, "At what point did Mr. Hornsby explain how the mental or infirmity or defect caused the defendant to not know what he was doing or not know it was wrong?"

The two questions are different, he said offering an example: If someone killed a person because they thought he was the Antichrist and was saving the world, it would be an example of someone who knew what they were doing but had the delusional belief that they were not doing anything wrong.

"But what are we talking about; did not know what he was doing or its consequences? There were no arguments connecting that defect to those issues.

"Weighing the evidence. As we start going through here, I wanted to remind the jury of something that the court said, that what the attorneys say is not evidence. So, when you're going back and you're listening to myself and also Mr. Hornsby, if something that was said is not how you remember it, you are the ones that make the determinations of what the evidence was.

"And there were multiple times where Mr. Hornsby kept on talking about he didn't have his Zoloft, didn't have his Zoloft. There's no Zoloft in this case. What the issue was, was whether or not he had the Lexapro. And those types of things."

He urged the jurors to look and listen closely at the testimony of both the lay and the expert witnesses.

"One of the examples I'm gonna give from there is John Anselmo when he would be talking, as he would be talking to you, he'd suddenly, aah, he was crying about Sue-Ellen, there wasn't a lot of tears. All right? That's an example of looking at the way somebody is saying, not only what they're saying, but how they're saying it.

"One of these things is, has the witness at some point said something inconsistent? An example of that is the Anselmo family lying here, that it has been portrayed to you is that Ian Anselmo's a child in a man's body. And all the family members came up and said it, they kept saying it, kept saying. But then, you know when I asked Rajko, 'Hey, I understand you're saying that today, but do you remember in a deposition saying something different about how he was not like that?' And it took me showing him his deposition to remind him that he actually denied that Ian was a child in a man's body back at that deposition. He said that, 'yeah, 'he would play with his toys but he wouldn't play with them in a childish way.'"

He said the state did not disagree that Ian had a mental illness, but there was disagreement about the diagnoses.

"Dr. Saunders talked about potentially needing to rule out schizoaffective disorder or schizophrenia.

We know that's actually been done now. Dr. Saunders said we can't do this at this time that he did the evaluation due to the defendant's age but he's had continuing appointments with Dr. DeLeon. Those have been ruled out. Schizotypal disorder has been disputed. Dr. Werner explained why that's not been appropriate."

He also touched on Dejah testifying that Ian talked to his toys,

"The important part, psychiatrically, is not that Ian talks to toys or Ian plays with toys. Psychiatrically what's important is when the toys talk back. And for seven years of treatment with Dr. DeLeon, there was never a single reference to that very important psychiatric type of symptom until Ian Anselmo is charged with murder.

"And you can see the records," he said. "…after being charged with second-degree murder, he goes to Dr. DeLeon and is like, 'You know what, this whole time my toys have been talking to me."

He also attacked the diagnosis of PTSD. "… you cannot eliminate the fact that the reason why he is suffering from PTSD is because he murdered his stepmom and is charged with second-degree murder. And the best evidence of that is prior to the murder, no PTSD. After the murder, PTSD. Now, PTSD is not a mental infirmity that led to this tragedy.

So, this is where the defense cannot meet their burden because of the condition he did not know what he was doing or its consequence. They have to prove that by clear and convincing evidence. And it's not a maybe. It's not a could be. It's not a probability.

"So, what is the *because*? The *because* is anger. The *because* is she did not do what he wanted. The *because* is he 'has no problem telling me he hates me.' The problem is *because* she was ruining the family. The *because* is he felt anger when he heard that his stepmother was definitely leaving. The *because* is Ian felt anger the moment his mother was minimizing the effects this had on his siblings.

"The defense tried to meet its burden and used Dr. Buffington, Dr. Saunders, Dr. DeLeon and family members."

The experts offered their opinions, he said.

"And everything that they talked about was maybe, could be, probably, because as Mr. Hornsby talked about a lot with Dr. Wener, this is 'soft science.' These are his words. Subject to interpretation. You can't do an objective test."

There is no test to determine if Ian is lying about not remembering the murder. It is normal for people in a traumatic event to block out such events, he said.

"They can't objectively tell you that is not what happened here. And they're the ones that have to prove it to you. So, these people are giving you maybes, could be's, probablies.
. ."

He talked about Buffington, saying "opinion based on bad information is a worthless opinion."

"Dr. Buffington says that Sue-Ellen took Ian's medications with her, including his Lexapro and Vyvanse, causing a sudden discontinuation for a period of time. Well, you have those text messages. They'll be back there with you. There is not a single reference in there that Sue-Ellen took those medicines. Nico wanted to tell you that that's in there. But even Mr. Hornsby corrected her. Now, it doesn't say that. I don't know why Dr. Buffington decided to say she took it when everyone was sitting there telling you that there's no evidence of that. But he chose to put that in his presentation.

"He also said that he was without his Lexapro and Vyvanse. And his basis for that information was the deposition of John Anselmo. Apparently, he did not do any other investigation…. "

Camuccio said once he got that information Buffington went into "school professor mode" and started talking about the effects of drug withdrawal. "Well, we know the basis of his opinion is flawed because first of all, Ian had his Vyvanse."

To prove his point, he played a video clip of Ian talking to the ambulance crew saying he had not taken his Lexapro for two to three days but adding, "I have my Vyvanse."

He reminded jurors that there had been testimony that Ian was never without his meds, but Ian told a nurse that sometimes he had to "wing it," while waiting for a refill.

"And he had all sorts of nice charts and graphs about all the different types of symptoms that would be found, and it's mostly what we've been talking about: flu-like symptoms, lethargy, insomnia." The one symptom that wasn't on the chart was violence.

"It's one thing to rely on bad information to form a bad opinion, he said. "It is quite another thing though to have information that goes against your opinion, reviewed it, and then act like it's not even there because it doesn't help your opinion."

He pointed out another serious flaw in Buffington's testimony. He discussed looking at the text messages between John and Sue-Ellen and the missing medications. But at one point, she says she left Vyvanse on the counter and that it should tide him over.

"Dr. Buffington may not have done a very good job of doing an investigation looking at those body-worn cameras. Maybe it wasn't provided to him, whatever it may be, we know he read those text messages as part of his opinion. But the fact that Ian actually did have access to Vyvanse, that's in those text messages, and then he puts it in his conclusions that not having Vyvanse exasperated this whole situation. I will leave it to you to determine what you should do when an expert does that. I would throw it out because you can't trust it. If you can't trust him on the little things, you can't trust him on the big ones.

"And avoiding the fact that Ian did, in fact, have his Vyvanse, which we know, because he tells the nurse, 'I have my Vyvanse, that's a pretty big thing."

He cautioned jurors about what they would see if they took copies of the text messages back to the jury room. Copies were color-coded and identified by the sender. "… there is no way of knowing for sure that that's not John typing away on there, but even if it is, when there's a discussion about Ian going from one mood to another you heard Dr. Werner describe to you how that is what manipulates Sue-Ellen. We will try one tactic. If that doesn't work, let me try something else."

Switching back to Buffington, he said that the legal definition of insanity states that even if there is prior mental illness, it must reach the level of the person not knowing it was wrong or realize the consequences.

Even if discontinuation syndrome caused diminished capacity, it is not insanity, he said.

Camuccio said Hornsby predicted that he would tell jurors that the case was not about John.

"I'm not saying that. I absolutely would agree that John Anselmo and his behaviors helped fuel the fire of what happened here today or happened on March 13th of 2019. That's not insanity.

"Whether or not the Anselmo clan is a cult is not insanity. Whether or not people were brainwashed is not insanity….

"This family dynamic that you have gotten an opportunity to see and hear from, they try to say we are this loving, caring family. I believe Nico was the one saying, 'I am in the most loving, caring home and why would I ever want to go out anywhere else but here?' But then in the same testimony talks about, 'no, I wasn't trying to strangle Dejah-Thoris. I was trying to gouge her eyes out.'

"Rajko talked, you saw the video where he was making threats to his mom. You heard testimony about strangling his mom. And then ultimately Ian Anselmo strangling and killing his mother.

"This family was brought up on violence. And they carried out violence. They preached loving and kindness, but they practiced hate. I agree with that. I agree that John Anselmo was where all of that started. But that's not insanity.

"None of that goes to whether or not Ian knew what he was doing or knew what he was doing was wrong when he was strangling his mother. Not a single bit of that upbringing brainwashing is insanity. It is because of orthodox religion, not insanity. Because of homeschooling, not insanity. Because they weren't property socialized, not insanity.

Because he's a child in a man's body, not insanity. Because it might be crazy, but that's not the same as insanity."

He explained that another portion of the insanity jury instruction states that unrestrained passion or ungoverned temper is not insanity, "even though the normal judgment of the person is overcome by passion or temper."

Ian said he was angry when Sue-Ellen minimized the effect her leaving would have on the children.

"Once again, the defense has to present you with evidence that Ian is simply saying 'I don't remember' is because of insanity. Ian not remembering it because of ungovernable temper or unrestrained passion is not insanity. That is one of the things that Dr. Werner told you was at play in this case because he could not be telling the truth about not remembering, but he could also have been overcome by this and therefore have the short-term amnesiac event as it relates to it."

There is no objective testing or evidence from Drs. Buffington, Saunders or DeLeon to prove their case, he said.

"Mr. Hornsby has gone after and attacked Dr. Werner about the testimony that she gives. And one of the things that he says is that she is the only person that told you that she could change her opinion if she got new information. My God! I hope so! If an expert will not change their opinion because they're presented with new evidence, potential evidence that their original opinion is wrong. Does that make them a better expert? That sounds like the type of person that's not doing it for a paycheck."

He said he would hope that all experts would do the same.

"He also tried to insinuate she had bias because of the cases she has testified in. But then she pointed out to him, actually the only other case I have with Mr. Camuccio right now, I'm hired by the defense. And his reaction was 'convenient.'

"Now, Dr. Werner talked to you about what was going on in this case. And despite the way Mr. Hornsby summarized her opinion and just said, well, the only reason why she said he was sane at the time of the offense is because of the short period of time that the psychotic event occurred. That was not what her testimony was."

What Werner was saying is that it is important to look at the things he said before and after the murder to see that he knew what he was doing was wrong.

"Mr. Hornsby also became very frustrated that she watched a two-minute video of Rajko behaving in a way that he said, 'That's crazy. Right? That's crazy. So, isn't he insane?' But they're not the same.

"And then he seems to get frustrated that Dr. Werner is saying that in order for me to make a determination about your new hypothetical, I would have to do a full evaluation. I would have to look at mental health records. I would have to go through and do my examination. And he's faulting her for doing what a psychiatric expert should do.

But the biggest part of that back and forth with Dr. Werner that I felt was important actually demonstrates how she dissects other pieces of information to talk about what really matters, and that's the *because*. Because as crazy as Mr. Hornsby wants to talk about the fact that this 10-year-old child wanted to kill his mother, the child also said, 'I would kill her but she's pregnant.' And you saw about a 15-second evaluation of how that statement shows that the child knew what he was doing was wrong. And that's important because that's showing that the *because* isn't there. That's why she said the things that she did.

"When the defendant first calls 911, he says, 'I accidentally killed someone.' He is aware of what he did. The defendant describes that happened before, during and after."

He then played the recording of the 911 call, including Ian saying, "I guess I strangled her," and "I'm so sorry I strangled her."

"What was going on immediately preceding the homicide? 'We got into an argument.' He very well may have depression, but he is aware of what is happening, and that's why they can't meet their burden of because.

He also played a clip of a female officer at the crime scene asking if he wants to sit up in case there are any ants in the area.

"That's the least of my worries right now, to be honest," Ian said.

He knows what he did and that it would have ramifications, Camuccio said.

He also said, "Daddy is going to be so pissed."

At the police department he said, "You can keep me here. I'm not trying to get out of anything."

"Once again, it's not enough to say there is evidence of mental illness. They have to connect the dots in such a way that it's clear and convincing. Such a way that is precise, explicit, lacking in confusion and of such weight that it produces a firm belief without hesitation in the matter at issue.

"And they have tried and failed to meet their burden through opinions where the experts are withholding information from and ignoring facts in evidence available to them. And there's body cameras and the statements about knowing what was happening in the car. 'We had an argument. I was angry.' And because of his anger, and because of his hatred, ill will, spite and evil intent. And that's why all of the problems [were caused] by John Anselmo's right-hand man.

"Ian, the defendant, on March 13, 2019, wanted to take his role as the second dad, or the hero of the story. He rushed out because he thought he was gonna convince Sue-Ellen, if not herself, to come back, but to get those kids. And when she said no, he hit her, broke her jaw, strangled her with a phone cord, strangled her with his bare hands, killing her and her unborn child. That's the *because.* That's why this happened.

"And the last fact that shows you that he knew what he was doing and knew what he was doing was wrong is the call that he makes to his dad on the day he was arrested. In that call, he tells his father she was ruining the family. This is motive. These are the thoughts in his head as to the why, the *because.*

Camuccio played a brief audio recording of the jail call.

"We were talking and we got into an argument.'

John Anselmo "But you're not supposed to kill her."

"I know. I'm sorry."

"You could go away."

"I know. I'm sorry."

"This wasn't because of depression. It wasn't because he didn't have his Lexapro for two days and was undergoing flu-like symptoms. He was angry. Strangled, killed his mother, extinguishing two lives.

"And the last bit I want to share and remind you another reason to show that none of the crazy, none of the SSRI, had anything to do with this was the first night that Sue-Ellen tried to escape, brought her children with her, went to her daughter's home, Dejah-Thoris. Before she ever took the pills, the defendant is banging on the door, angry, trying to get those kids back (and making threats, Dolan testified).

"The state has met its burden. We have proved beyond a reasonable doubt he strangled, killed his mother because of hatred, ill will, evil intent, and thereby killing the unborn child that she was carrying. The defense cannot meet their burden. And it's as Mr. Hornsby said, and the judge has told you, that sympathy should play no part in your verdict.

"Just as sympathy should not be taken into consideration because two lives were extinguished, you should hold me to my burden, that we've proven that. Sympathy should not be part of that.

"But it also should not be part of the determination of whether they proved what they needed to prove, because they can't. Because he was sane. Thank you."

CHAPTER 27

THE VERDICT

The higher the stakes the faster the heartbeat, and that is never more true than in a trial, especially a murder case when a verdict comes in.

Bailiffs, on high alert when a verdict is about to be announced, stand in the center aisle to keep families from attacking each other or rushing the defendant, the lawyers or the judge.

Often, family members hold hands as if they are at the highest point on a roller coaster and are about to take the plunge.

The jury wasn't out long before sending a note requesting to the judge. They wanted to hear a recording of the 911 call again. This was potentially good news for Camuccio, who in his closing pointed to statements Ian made that showed he knew what he had done.

Four hours after hearing the 10-minute recording, they sent another note.

"The bailiff informed me there's a note," Judge Welke told the lawyers. "Oh, it says the vote is complete."

"Oh Jesus," Camuccio exclaimed.

Within about four minutes, family, friends and spectators were allowed back in the courtroom.

"I know many of you have been here all week. I know this has been very emotional. I don't know which way the verdict will go. But regardless, I just ask that there not be any outbursts. Just let the verdict be read and we'll go with that," the judge said.

Dejah, her grandparents, mother-in-law, Dolan and others sat quietly on the courtroom bench seats behind the prosecutors' table. They seemed nervous, pale and wounded.

John, dressed in his trademark back clothing, was two rows behind Ian, holding Rajko's hand.

Ian sat next to Hornsby at the defense table, his head bowed slightly, his hands resting on his knees.

The judge checked the verdict form, then passed it to the clerk so she could read it. He then had Ian and Hornsby stand. Ian, his long black hair tied in a thick ponytail, stood motionless and without emotion as the verdict was read. Hornsby bowed his head as if to let the bad news wash over him.

"In the circuit court of the Fifth Judicial Circuit of the state of Florida versus Ian Magnus Anselmo, case number 2019-CF-751, verdict count one, we the jury find as follows as to count one of the charge: The defendant is guilty of murder in the second-degree. So say we all, dated this 12th day of April, 2024. Dennis Denlinger foreperson."

The clerk continued, announcing that he had also been found guilty of second-degree murder "of an unborn child by injury to the mother."

John and Rajko left before bailiffs led Ian to the front of the courtroom to be fingerprinted and led to the jail.

"When it was over, Cindy Miller, wearing a green ribbon and a bright crystal she said represented her daughter's smile, was bathed in bright TV news lights as she prepared to speak.

She repeated the fact that she had forgiven Ian and that it was "very sad" that Ian would spend the rest of his life behind bars.

However, she let it be known that she was not happy with the testimony of John and the children.

"A lot of it was not true, and it made my daughter look really bad, and that's not the person she was. She was beautiful. She was Miss Eustis and Miss Teen Lake County and was very talented. She was a very popular hairstylist in Eustis."

She said Sue-Ellen had lots of friends, "and all these things about her mental illness and drinking, I don't know where he came up with that."

Other family members greeted each other and spoke in hushed tones.

Dejah sat in a chair, doubled over, sobbing.

"She doesn't have anything to say," said her mother-in-law, who draped her arm around her.

CHAPTER 28

"SHE TRUSTED HIM"

Sentencing was supposed to take place on July 23, but Camuccio pulled a rabbit out of the hat to counter Hornsby's motion for leniency, so the hearing was moved to Oct. 18, 2024.

Among Hornsby's arguments was that Ian's young emotional age made him incapable of realizing the consequences. He also cited case law about a defendant's "unsophisticated" manner of homicide. He wrote that "attempting to choke someone can be considered an unsophisticated act."

He also claimed Anselmo had expressed remorse, but Camuccio produced a recording of a jail call in July after the trial from Ian to his father, where he could be heard saying: "What I did was not intentional but there were benefits."[70]

Judge Brian Welke delayed sentencing until Oct. 18 so Hornsby could review all jail calls.

---

70. Trial transcript, Vol. IX, April 12, 2024.

DEJAH'S HEARTBREAK

There is always an underlying current of anxiety, sadness and anger on sentencing days. Friends and family would audibly groan if allowed. There is an emotional pop-off valve, however through victim impact statements.

Dejah's was heart-breaking.

"It is with tremendous pain and sorrow that I make this statement to the members of the court today, and as I read this, I am reminded of what should have been but never will be.

"I am Dejah-Thoris Waite, the stepsister of Ian, and the daughter of Sue-Ellen. I've had five years to think about what I would say at this moment, but no time can ever really prepare you for this. The horror I've had to live through the past five years and all I can do is keep asking myself how did it come to this?

"The trial did not truly give this courtroom an idea of how this has impacted me and I had no choice but to defend myself or my mother. "I lost my whole family, my brother, Ian, and worst of all, my mom. You see, when I ran away, I tried to maintain contact with my siblings but I had to constantly agree to a different deal, do something a specific way, just to speak to them. Simply having a boyfriend, who… has now been my husband of seven years, was an absolute no if I ever wanted to see my siblings.

"The same sister who claims that she wants to gouge my eyes out on the stand was the only person I told of my plans to even leave the house, Sitting in the garage in trouble one night, in the pitch blackness on the cold concrete floor, we would use a small, little orange light on the deep freezer to check for roaches and spiders. She used my lap as a pillow and I told her that I was going to be leaving and do what

I could to see her again one day. And the same sister was supportive and excited for me and told me to get married. But now she wants to kill me.

"Korak was that sibling that I took a special bond to, and it was a motherly bond because of the drastic age difference, but I never did tell him to call him mommy. This was farfetched and just one of the many things said during the trial that didn't have any truth. He was my baby brother who liked to follow me around and would rather help me clean the house than play. He was my whole heart and a sorrow that I felt for leaving the day I left was so immense I felt like I couldn't breathe.

"Rajko used to do puzzles with me. Every morning, he would give me a big hug and tell me how he loved me. And he was one of the sweetest toddlers that you would have ever met.

"Tars lit up our world. Ian would hold him as much of the day as he could and Tars would see him, would smile just seeing us around him.

"Eric, I get the pleasure of having a relationship with now. But watching what he has come through could bring me to tears. He has come so far and is now doing amazing things, living an amazing life.

"Grey was just one of the little babies when I left. But seeing him and Moe the week that my mother left home, they were in my home. I wish desperately that I could see them again. I hate that they will never remember their mother and they are being told things that aren't true about her. For anyone to believe she was a maniac is absolutely absurd. But sure enough, the kids in the house will."

She noted that she is a registered nurse and premed student and has studied mental illness as part of her training.

"… research shows schizotypal, ADHD, personality disorders have extremely strong genetic components. Of the four oldest children, I was the only one to never see a psychiatrist or be medicated at any point in my entire life. I am also the only child who was my mother's biological and not Johnny's. The three others who share DNA with my mother have all seen a psychiatrist and have been diagnosed with some sort of illness at some point.

"My mother was not mentally ill. Even five years later, emails are being sent out with my mother's mental health records to me, and Nico is sure to say, 'You're nothing but a manipulator and a parasite to me.' Anyone who knows me wouldn't describe me with either of those words, but the name-calling, which was common in our household, I want to point to because it's exactly what my mother went through. When you are called the same names over and over again you do eventually believe them.

"Still, we're being tormented by this tragedy. During these five years, my flowers were removed from her grave. My mother was dug back up to be cremated so I couldn't visit her resting spot.

"Emails are sent out trying to degrade her character. I've been told I'm the one who killed my mother. I'm told that I have bad-mouthed Ian. But the truth is, only I know what I actually did during those first few months. Both my Granny and I defended Ian. We commented back to strangers who said terrible things about both him and my mother. We deleted those who pushed for a death penalty.

"At the time of the event we couldn't have been more sympathetic. If Ian only knew how devastated we were about him too, how we grieved and prayed for him. As this case has continued, we have learned a lot more about what really happened, and as much as we still try to keep negativity surrounding Ian out of our mouths and others' we now understand the extent of the crime that he committed and we would just like Sue-Ellen to be at peace, as well as us."

She talked about how close she had been to Ian, not only in age, but spending every day with each other and sharing child-rearing duties.

She repeated what she said in her deposition about how they would spend hours entertaining the younger children and each other, and how she thought he was the funniest person she had ever known.

"If you asked me what I had to say about Ian had this never happened, I would have told you he was the only one who always had my back. I would drink a glass of chocolate milk in the morning for breakfast, and if we didn't have enough milk for myself and everyone else's cereal, then I would go without. If Ian noticed, he would ask if I had my milk, and if I didn't, he would eat his cereal dry or use the water instead."

She said he was her best friend. "I did everything I could to keep him out of trouble. So much so that I would bend the stories and diffuse the situations as best I could with our other siblings just to avoid bringing it to our dad. My other siblings often said I took favor with Ian, and I did. I loved Ian.

"Ian didn't have patience with people. He was short-tempered. He was not quick to admit he was wrong.

"He wasn't a people person. He would joke that he liked our brothers and sisters before they could talk, and once they started talking, not so much. But let's be honest, when you're 16 years old you don't always want to babysit five kids. And now I see that's not abnormal or wrong.

"But Ian never got impatient with me. I feel like I saw another side of him. The goofy side, the smart side, the loyal side. I feel like he would defend me in a heartbeat and he always had my back.

"I cannot say the same about him with anyone else, but for me, I knew the Ian I felt like no one got to see. That's what I would have told if you had asked me about him and this had never happened."

She talked about the letter she wrote to her mother, and how it took years for her to get up the nerve to do it.

"I was discouraged to have contact with just my mother. I would write her happy birthday, happy Mother's Day. I sent flowers to her work. And I tried asking her to lunch, but I received a message asking why I was trying to get her alone. My mother was scared about the flowers and getting in trouble about them and messaged me to please stop. I was in fear of her being reprimanded for talking to me, I ceased communication for some time.

"I had gained enough courage to write her and I left a letter on her desk and I never thought by doing that I would be here today. Hearing from her was one of the most exciting days of my life at that point, and it was so short-lived."

She talked about getting the call about the attack from Dolan while working as a waitress.

"I thought in my mind she had been beaten up. I thought that she would be so upset because she was so beautiful, and I was hoping it wasn't her face. I thought maybe she had internal bleeding and might need surgery."

She said when she arrived at the hospital with her grandmother, "I was yelled at by John and our families were separated."

When the doctor told her Sue-Ellen was not going to make it, she fell backwards from her chair, hit the floor and sobbed.

"I felt like my world was spinning. They transferred her to Orlando and it was then that the news came out saying it was Ian who called 911 and that he had killed her. And I couldn't even believe it.

"My Granny and I went to Orlando and I called each of my uncles to explain the news and my mother's best friend. Making those calls and hearing the raw emotion of a family member being told what was happening to their sister or best friend will haunt me forever. And the emotional scars that I have from that day are never gonna go away.

"When we got to the hospital, John would not let us see my mom. We slept the night in the lobby. And by morning, new security saw that my mom had gone to a divorce lawyer the day before the attack and felt it was not right to have the man she was trying to leave in the room.

"When I saw he for the first time, my mother [was] laying there on the stretcher in a neck brace, bruised, swollen, dried blood all over her. Her baby still with a heartbeat fluttering in her tummy, laying there motionless, [was] being forced to breathe with a machine. Her blonde hair was stained with red blood. How do you even react to seeing your mother like this?

"The day they told me that there was no way she would make it, I drove home alone, a good hour, hour-and-a-half, and the last song I listened to was Adele's 'Set Fire to the Rain.' And it may not mean anything to most people, but I cried harder than I thought possible, and I won't ever forget the deepest sorrow that I've ever felt. I thought I was going to stop breathing.

"I pulled into the driveway and I had to collect myself and walk in on our kids, my brothers in the house, with no idea what was going on with their mom.

"I've consulted multiple doctors and read through multiple trials and research studies trying to keep the baby alive and I was told countless times there was no way. I searched and I searched. But when they called and told me she had gone brain dead and it was over and time to come say goodbye, we had no choice in the matter anymore."

She said the months and years afterward were filled with grievous surprises.

"I didn't expect my flowers to be moved. I didn't expect her to be dug back up. I didn't expect the emotions that followed, knowing it was Ian who did this. I've kicked myself for years, even before the murder of Sue-Ellen, for not telling Ian that I was running away and asking if he wanted to come with me. I debated it all through the night before I ran away that morning, but I let my fear of him talking me out of it, or possibly telling our father, keep me from asking him.

"But at one point, he too wanted to run away and was going to live in the woods and write me. And I blamed myself. I felt like this was my fault. I should have never written to her. I should have had Ian run away with me. I was angry with God, and I didn't understand how someone so amazing could die in such a terrible way.

"And what wasn't shown in court were all the pictures and videos that I have of the kids playing and laughing. I still have the cardboard box Korak and I made a house out of while my mom took pictures of us. The kids drowned my husband in teddy bears on the couch. My mother cooked dinner for us and the kids and always fed Tars before she ate."

She then made the painful observation that all victims' families make about trials and the important thing that is overlooked.

"This whole case has been focused on Ian and to prove this or that, but who's the victim? My mother. My mommy."

She said her mother's very presence comforted her. "Looking at her made me happy. She always smelled good. And when I smell the moisturizer brand she used or the laundry detergent or white comforter, the shampoo, even now it still makes me happy like it used to.

"And what the court didn't get to see are the beautiful pictures of Sue-Ellen, the pictures of her holding her children, of all the stories she would tell her clients. How she gushed every time she had another baby. How bragging about us was her favorite pastime. How she touched dozens of lives throughout her lifetime. How she inspired others and showed them they were special.

"The court didn't get to see how I've had to watch the person who means so much to me, my Granny, have to stay strong because she lost her daughter. Her daughter, her baby, her firstborn. And I can't even fathom losing one of my girls. That's what the court didn't get to see.

"And in this court, my mother was just the victim and her character was only degraded. She isn't just a body that had something terrible done to it. She was a person who meant something to so many people. She was a mother to nine children, pregnant with another."

"My mother was a beauty pageant winner and used to sing as her talent. Her voice was more beautiful than you could imagine…. And she used to sing to Nico and me, 'Somewhere Over the Rainbow,' and now I sing it to my girls.

"I've had to come to grips with the fact that Ian killed her. He wasn't the Ian that I remembered when I left home. And I've had to separate that in my mind.

"And some in this courtroom have tried to tear my mother to pieces and I'll be damned if someone did that to me and didn't defend how great of a mother I truly was, so you'd best bet I'm about to do it for her.

"I wish I could remind Ian of all the truths and memories that have been suppressed and slowly erased. Sue-Ellen was not a detached person. She used to have Mondays off from work and we loved it when it was her day to pick us up from school. She would bring us home and sit us up on the high-top counter while she was preparing dinner to quiz us on our spelling words. If we didn't have her quiz us, we had to write every single word 20 times. But when Mommy was home, we only wrote the words we got wrong when she quizzed us, and we loved that.

"She used to pack our lunches every day in elementary school without fail, except for nacho chili cheese day where we would beg that she give us money to eat in the cafeteria. And. of course, she always did.

"When we were in middle school, we used to take Eric and Nico to the elementary school and then do something with Ian and me until middle school started. Driving around to different neighborhoods, looking at the beautiful houses or getting us a Yoo-Hoo, which was our favorite. We used to save the caps and collect them.

"When we started doing virtual school, she would try to actively participate, taking the time to research places to take us on field trips and come up with ways to incorporate it into our studies. And then Sundays after church, she would make a big brunch for us to eat. And she was a really good cook. She made everything from scratch. Always homemade spaghetti sauce, never from the jar. And big debate of sugar in spaghetti sauce? The Answer is yes.

"On days she worked late, I would cook dinner, but I was only allowed to use the microwave. On Fridays we didn't eat meat for religious reasons, so I would prep the kitchen for my mom to make tuna melts since you can't make that in the microwave, at least not very well. And she would come home from over 10-hour long days on her feet as a cosmetologist, and oftentimes pregnant or having just had a baby, and still make all of us tuna melts with mac and cheese as a side. And it sounds trivial but that was one of our favorites."

Saturday night was movie night. "My mom loved the old black and white detective movies and she would fix us some brownies and ice cream and the whole family would sit together and watch a movie. Sherlock Holmes, Charlie Chan, Mr. Moto were among our favorites."

She said her mother bottle-fed the babies, getting up every three hours.

"I wish so badly I could explain to my siblings that when we were told our mother didn't love us because she wanted to get lunch with a group of friends once a month, that this was not unusual. That being so exhausted when she got home that she needed a minute to sit down and change into comfortable clothes is not unusual.

"Her wanting to buy a nice pair of jeans that was talked about like it was the end of the world is not unusual. We had more toys than we knew what to do with. And I promise, the $200 she may have spent one time on a pair of jeans that would have lasted her years wasn't gonna affect us and sure didn't mean that she didn't love us.

"And since everyone in that house wants to bring up that Mommy used to sit on the couch and eat ice, as if that was her being lazy after working long hours, that is a sign of anemia, which causes extreme exhaustion on top of how hard she was already working to support the entire family, in our big house, as a single income provider."

Dejah cited her work as a nurse and the things she has learned working in labor and delivery and OB/GYN. "Pregnancy and motherhood is my passion, my academic interest, and I can't even express the toll that time would take on a mother physically, emotionally and mentally."

"Our father would provoke her, would pit Ian or me against her time and time again. And to endure this physical and emotional abuse during such a vulnerable time as pregnancy or soon after delivery is unimaginable to me. The strength it would have taken our mom to get up every morning and continue to provide for us is much more than we can understand and far more than any of those kids could ever understand because they've never even had a job.

"If Mommy was as mentally ill as our father tried to make us believe, she would have never been a successful cosmetologist, to be able to financially support a family of so many children. She wouldn't have had such a huge support system with hundreds of friends and clients who have only good things to say about her before and after her death.

"My mother was beautiful, smart and maternal. She did not deserve the life that she lived. And I believe the evidence presented in trial speaks for itself of the stories that could be told of what happened to my mother, me, and my siblings. It would accomplish nothing to recount the trauma that still gives me nightmares to this day. It won't change what happened.

She said Sue-Ellen was torn between wanting to come to a family pizza party to celebrate Ian's book being published or keeping her distance. John and Ian pressured her to come.

"Ian tried to speak with her on multiple occasions, yet she was afraid. She wanted desperately to go to that party …. She cried that night because she felt so bad, but she was so scared. And because we are here today, I'd say that her fear was not misplaced.

"The sheer brutality of this murder takes my breath away, and that Ian could have possibly done this. This was not a quick death or a reaction like shooting a gun. To strangle someone to the point of death, you slowly watch their life fade away.

"Evidence showed both manual strangulation and cord strangulation. She struggled. She was beaten and strangled."

"I wish that I could rewind time. My heart hurts more than I thought was possible and it feels like a nightmare.

"I lost all my siblings because I wanted a better life. I grieved for years and still do and then this happened. I'll forever mourn for the fear that she felt while she was dying. I will forever wonder what she said, how she fought and why she wasn't able to get away. Why couldn't Ian have just walked away? Even if he had hit her out of anger, she would have let it go. How could he possibly have taken it so far, to slowly take the life out of her, and even knowing that she was pregnant. She still had decades to live and she never deserved to be killed by someone claiming to love her.

"She trusted him. She met with him and he killed her.

"My children won't have her as a grandmother. I don't get to have that experience of calling my mother when I'm in labor, of seeing the joy in her face as she gets to hold her grandbaby. Having my mother hold my hand while I go through postpartum. Getting to call my mom when I'm sad and need to talk. When I need parenting advice. When I want to gush about something cute that my 1-year-old did. To be there at my RN graduation. To share my excitement getting into medical school. I will never have my mother again.

"I never got to take my mother out to eat. I'll never get to get my nails done with my mom. We had planned a whole day for the day after she was attacked to go shopping, but we didn't get to do it. I wanted to finally get that experience with her like I remembered as a kid. Before she was with my stepdad, she took me to the mall every Friday and we split a Cinnabon. Every Monday after the YMCA she would buy a shrimp cocktail platter and split it with me.

"I never felt like my mother didn't care. I don't have a single bad memory with my mother. She never hurt me. I miss her so bad that it hurts. And I miss the fact that I had another sibling that is now dead. And I just wish this nightmare would go away but it won't.

"God knows the truth of what has happened in that household and what happened that day. God knows what my mother had been through what courage and strength she had and I don't know why she's gone now. But my family and I know that my mother is no longer in pain, as there are no tears in heaven, and that she's raising her baby up there.

"Let the court know my mother deserves justice. And may God have mercy on Ian and change his mind and heart as time goes on, in *Deorum nomine* (in God's name).

CHAPTER 29

"NO TEARS IN HEAVEN"

Sue-Ellen's mother, Cindy Miller, is a gentle, kind, soft-spoken woman, but beneath that exterior is a combination of grit, love, and Christian forgiveness, and she showed it when she stood at the podium to give her victim impact statement.

"This is one of the hardest things I have ever had to do. How do you say in a few minutes how the murder of your only daughter has impacted your life?"[71]

"All of my life I dreamed of having a daughter. Sue-Ellen was my firstborn child and I was so excited when she was born. That was one of the happiest days of my life. She was a beautiful baby and I had great hope for her future.

"Sue-Ellen was a smart, strong-willed, independent child. As she grew up, we discovered that she had a beautiful singing voice. She loved singing at church, community events and weddings. Sue-Ellen was Miss Teen Lake County, Miss Eustis Teen, Miss Eustis, and America's Little Darling.

---

71. Trial transcript, Oct. 18, 2024.

"She had a great sense of style and she was an extremely successful hairdresser for over 20 years. Sue-Ellen was the girl in the room who was always noticed. She was almost always the prettiest girl in the room, yet she made everyone else feel special when she lit up the room with her dazzling smile.

Along with her beautiful smile, she had the most beautiful blue eyes and a gorgeous fair complexion. Sue-Ellen was the daughter I longed for all of my life, and I loved her with all of my life.

"Sue-Ellen married young and had a baby girl. Unfortunately, my daughter's first husband developed an addiction problem. Sue-Ellen tried to work things out, but she ended up getting a divorce.

"After remaining single for several years, she ran into an old friend from her high school days. He had been married and had custody of his three children. I knew him and his children because the two older children, one of whom was Ian, attended the school where I was working. The children were smart and well-mannered. Their father was very attentive to them and he was very polite and kind when he was at the school.

"When he and Sue-Ellen developed a relationship, I was very happy about it. He was charming and treated Sue-Ellen and my granddaughter well. They had a beautiful wedding and I had never seen Sue-Ellen so happy as she was on her wedding day.

"Things seemed to be going well in the beginning, but over the years it became more apparent that Sue-Ellen was in a dysfunctional, manipulative relationship. There were many times during her marriage that my husband and I were not allowed to see her or our grandchildren.

"Sue-Ellen desperately wanted me to have a good relationship with her husband, but unfortunately, that was not possible. Eventually I was not able to see her at all. We did not see or talk to each other for over two years before she left her husband. Sue-Ellen was also not able to spend time with friends, family or anyone except her husband and children outside of her workplace.

"On March 6, 2019, Sue-Ellen left her husband after 13 years of marriage. She took her minor children and moved in with her daughter. The following morning my husband Jack and I were able to see and talk to Sue-Ellen and our grandchildren for the first time in over two years. One of them was only 20 months old and we had never seen him. I had only seen her next-to-the-youngest child once and that was at the hospital on the day he was born.

"During the next week, I was able to babysit for my grandchildren and talk with my daughter. Many positive things happened during that first week after my daughter left. Her customers who knew that she had left her husband were giving her extremely large tips. One of the managers at a store where she shopped told her that she used to notice how her husband treated her at the store and gave her a discount on the things she needed for the kids.

"When Sue-Ellen would come home at the end of each day, she would say, 'Let me tell you about the God things that happened to today.' Then, she would tell me about the generosity and kindness of her customers, friends, and even strangers like the store manager.

"The best thing was that she he had no idea that anyone had been aware of how she had been treated over the years, or that anyone cared about her. Now, she was learning that she was loved by so many and that she would have people to help her.

"During the week before the attack, Sue-Ellen and I were able to discuss her plans for the future. She talked about taking care of her new baby and buying a new home in a gated community where she could feel safe. Sue-Ellen wanted her children to attend school. She wanted her son, who has Down syndrome, to go to Lake Hills School where he could have friends and receive the therapies that he needs. She desperately needed a more dependable car, so that was the first thing on her list of things to do.

"When Sue-Ellen left her husband, the situation was very volatile, so she wanted to move to my house with her children after things calmed down to a point where she and I both felt that it would be safe for her to do so. That would give her time to save money and be able to build a new life for herself and her children.

"Six days after she left, Sue-Ellen met with and hired a divorce attorney. Sue-Ellen was very happy, hopeful and excited when she got home that night. She loved the attorney and she felt like things were starting to look up for her.

"I will never forget how beautiful she looked when she got home that night. One of my biggest regrets is that I didn't take her picture before I left that evening, but I had no idea that I would never see her conscious again.

"The following day, I was babysitting for my grandchildren when I received a call from my husband Jack. The police had come to our house to tell him that our daughter had been attacked and that he needed to go to the hospital. That was all he knew. In my mind I was thinking that maybe she was bruised and maybe had a broken arm or something. I immediately picked up my granddaughter at her job and went to the hospital.

"When we got to the hospital, the valet loop was filled with police cars. I was hoping that they were not there because of what had happened to Sue-Ellen. We were told that the emergency room was on lockdown and we were taken to a waiting area. We still did not know what had happened or who had attacked my daughter, and one of the police officers or the hospital personnel could tell us anything.

"Finally, a very kind, young doctor walked over to me and said, 'Are you Sue-Ellen's mother?' He sat down next to me and held my hand. I immediately knew that meant that the news was not going to be good. He explained that the first people on the scene thought that she was dead, but the emergency medical personnel had found a very faint heartbeat. He said that she had been strangled and had an anoxic brain injury and she was going to be transported to Orlando Regional Medical Center.

Then the police came over to tell us that they had arrested Sue-Ellen's stepson, Ian, for the attack.

"Our family sat by Sue-Ellen's bedside in Orlando for the next five days as she drifted away. We had the privilege to be there to express our love and goodbyes as her heart gradually stopped beating.

"It is strange, but as she lay dying, in my mind, she became my baby and my little girl all over again. I saw her as a newborn baby in my arms, the toddler taking her first steps, the headstrong child who wanted to do everything her way. The little baton twirler. The girl who always had a unique sense of style. The loving sister to her three brothers. And gorgeous beauty queen with the voice of an angel.

"Sue-Ellen will forever be the beautiful daughter that I longed for all my life. I will never forget kissing her beautiful face one last time and glancing back from the doorway of the hospital room to get one last look at her. That was the worst day of my life.

"My family experienced the result of evil. There are no words to explain evil. I have been dreading today. It has now been five-and-a-half years since Sue-Ellen was killed. To some people, her death has become old news. To others, it was a sad dip in the road on their journey. I feel as though I didn't just hit a bump, but I was detoured to a whole new road. It is a road that I didn't want to travel. It is unfamiliar and scary sometimes.

"I am so thankful that I always have God's love and promises to guide me down this road. I also have the joy of the Lord and peace. That doesn't mean that I don't still have sadness over the loss of my daughter. Grief washes over me like a wave sometimes and I suppose it always will. It is cleansing and good to cry and be sad for a while. I am thankful that I don't have to dwell in sorrow over my circumstances because I know my daughter is in heaven. There are no tears in heaven. There is no evil in heaven. I know that she is experiencing unimaginable peace, love and joy. That is what I always wanted for her and that brings me joy, too.

I want to make sure that people don't forget about her unborn baby. She was already making plans for how she was going to take care of the baby. She was hoping that this baby would be a girl. Sue-Ellen said that she was going to raise this baby her way.

Her unborn baby would be turning five years old next month. We figured out that the baby's due date would have been Nov. 6 and we recognize that day as the baby's birthday every year. The day the baby would have been born in 2019 we put a flower on Sue-Ellen's station at the salon in the baby's honor. I have acknowledged the baby's birthday in some way ever since then.

"I also have a small statue of a baby resting in the palm of God's hand in one of my flower beds. It is a place where I can go to remember the grandchild that I never got to meet here on Earth.

"Unfortunately, I have also been unable to have a relationship with Sue-Ellen's minor children since her death. I have had to grieve over losing those grandchildren as well.

"As I was walking down the hospital corridor to go home on the day that she died, I was thinking about walking into a world where Sue-Ellen would no longer exist. My greatest desire was to do whatever I could to make sure she would leave a great legacy and would not be forgotten.

"Everything that God allows in your life, He will use for good. In Romans 8:28, God says, "and we know that all things work together for good to those who love God, to those who are called according to his purpose.'

"I knew that Sue-Ellen's death was not part of God's will because it was meant for evil. But I also knew that God could use her death for good. When Sue-Ellen died, I prayed that God would use her death for good and for His glory. God has answered my prayer by using her story and her memory in a mighty way.

"Within a week, I had two people send me messages about how they had a family member who had decided to leave an abusive relationship because of what happened to Sue-Ellen.

"Over the past five years, I have had more people let me know that Sue-Ellen's story had given them the courage to leave a potentially dangerous situation. One of them had a stepson that she lived in fear of. She said she was praying about what to do and God put Sue-Ellen on her mind. She left her husband soon after that.

"I have had people who I have never met contact me about their dysfunctional situations, and I have had the opportunity to encourage them and pray for them. Her death has not been in vain because her story has helped so many other women.

Another important part of Sue-Ellen's legacy is that we were able to start the Sue-Ellen Miller Anselmo Memorial Scholarship for cosmetology at Lake Technical College. Since the scholarship's inception in 2019, 11 students have received the scholarship thanks to the generosity of her family and friends.

"I read that pain is a microphone and that God does not waste pain. I have found this to be true. Sue-Ellen's murder caused people to be a lot more interested in what I have to say. The greatest way that God has been glorified through this tragedy is that I have become much bolder about sharing what the Lord has done for me, and people actually want to know how God has strengthened me to carry on. God has given me the opportunity to share the Gospel and the healing power of forgiveness countless times through Sue-Ellen's story.

"I know that Sue-Ellen and her baby are in heaven, I also believe that her greatest wish would be that all of you would someday be there too. The good news is that grace and mercy are offered to us from God, free for the asking. We are all sinners. Our sins separate us from God. But He loves us so much that he sent His son to die for the forgiveness of our sins.

"If any of you haven't already done so, please confess your sins to God. Tell him that you believe that Jesus died to pay the debt for your sins and tell him that you want to give your life for him. The good news for all of us is that our sins, no matter how terrible we think they are, do not define our future. God loves us and he wants us to spend eternity with Him.

"I believe that Sue-Ellen would want her greatest legacy to be that other people came to know God's love and forgiveness because of what happened to her.

"I was actually very sad when I found out that Ian had killed Sue-Ellen. I think it would have been easier if her killer had been a stranger. I have known Ian since he was in the first grade. When Sue-Ellen married his father, I considered him to be my grandson. He came to my home many times when he was a child. He celebrated holidays in my home. We made gingerbread houses together, made crafts together, played at the park together, and shared meals together.

"Sue-Ellen loved Ian. In the last text on her phone, she and Ian said 'I love you' to each other. I can't imagine the betrayal that she must have felt when he was killing her the same afternoon that he texted that he loved her.

"Ian is very smart and he had so much promise. His future was always bright and he had accomplished a great deal during the almost 21 years before he killed my daughter and unborn grandchild.

"If you were at the trial, you were given a small glimpse into the lives of the children and the home. It is a life where the love of their father is conditional and has to be earned. The children tend to do what they believe will please their father in order to earn his favor. I truly believe that part of the reason that Ian killed Sue-Ellen was because he thought that Sue-Ellen had hurt his father.

"I would imagine that Ian doesn't know much about receiving unconditional love from his earthly father, so it is probably hard for him to understand the unconditional love that his heavenly father has for him. I want Ian to know that before Jesus died on the cross for his sins, he already knew what those sins were going to be. He loved him enough to die anyway.

"Most everyone is familiar with John 3:16. 'For God so loved the world, that he gave his only begotten Son, whosoever so believeth in him should not perish, but have everlasting life.' Most people are not as familiar with the following verse, John 3:17. 'For God sent not his Son into the world to condemn the world, but that the world through him might be saved.'

"I don't want to live under condemnation. I want him to live in God's love and forgiveness. I truly hope that Ian will ask God for forgiveness and give his life to him. I believe Ian can still be used in a great way while he is in prison.

"While Sue-Ellen was in the hospital I decided that I was going to forgive Ian. That set us free to be able to see how her death could be used for God's glory and it freed me from letting hatred and bitterness ruin my life.

"Unfortunately, justice means that there are consequences that will have to be paid here on Earth. No outcome can bring about a happy ending to this story. But Sue-Ellen and my unborn grandchild deserve justice. I forgave Ian the night I learned he was her attacker and I wish him no ill will. However, Ian brutally killed my daughter, and he has to face the consequences for his crime.

"I know this but it has brought me nothing but sadness to see him searched, fingerprinted, and taken to jail after the guilty verdict was read. I have no doubt that if Ian had not killed my beautiful daughter and her baby, he would have had the opportunity to have an immensely successful future.

"The truth is though, that he did take their lives and their futures. It truly breaks my heart to know that justice on Earth can only be served by Ian spending a long prison sentence. I will continue to pray for Ian's safety, his salvation, and that he will be able to live out God's purpose for his life. Thank you."

CHAPTER 30

"HATED, EVIL, ILL WILL, SPITE"

The gut-wrenching, heart-felt words of Cindy Miller and Dejah's impact statements were still echoing in the minds of those sitting motionless in the courtroom when the lawyers flexed their vocal cords for the sentencing arguments to come.

Soon, it would be Ian's chance to speak, and his take would be stunning. Equally stunning would be the recordings of two jail calls.

Florida utilizes a sentencing scoresheet compiled by the state's Department of Corrections, taking into consideration such things as prior convictions. Ian, of course, had no priors.

In Ian's case, the lowest possible sentence would have been 447 months, Camuccio said.

Hornsby, pointing to the statutes, objected to the way the state added up points for the death of the unborn child. "And

I'm just making this legal objection, judge. I'm leaving the moral argument out of it."[72]

He admitted that his argument "doesn't really affect how the scoresheet is interpreted at the end."

The judge said he would look at the statute.

Hornsby also referred to his motion for downward departure of sentence and said that to "make the sentencing simpler," he was eliminating number four of the five-point motion. That point contended that "the offense was committed in an unsophisticated manner and was an isolated incident for which the defendant has shown remorse."

There was some other legal quibbling until Hornsby announced that Ian wanted to speak.

He did not say why. However, he said he would make arguments for the other four:

- "The capacity of the defendant to appreciate the criminal nature of the conduct or to conform that conduct to the requirements of law was substantially impaired."

- "The defendant requires specialized treatment for a mental disorder that is unrelated to substance abuse or addiction or for a physical disability, and the defendant is amenable to treatment."

- "The defendant acted under extreme duress or under the domination of another person."

- "At the time of the offense the defendant was too young to appreciate the consequences of the offense."

---

72. Trial transcripts, Oct. 18, 2024.

There was some other legal quibbling until Hornsby announced that Ian wanted to speak.

REMORSE?

"Your honor, before I begin, please allow me to preface by saying I was not aware I was going to have to defend myself today until the eleventh hour. Only on Tuesday (two days earlier) did Mr. Hornsby inform me [of] that, contrary to what he told me and the court…. He has not been listening to all my previous jail calls in an attempt to provide context for what I said in the clips that you will hear. He then went on to say that he wasn't going to defend me today. I would have to do it myself.

"I want this latest display of unprofessionalism and dishonesty on Mr. Hornsby's part to be on the record.

"All that being said, I would like you to please look past my awkwardness and strange delivery and to take into account that I am autistic with a genius IQ but the emotional maturity of an 11-year-old, and that I am mentally ill. I'm not on most of my medications, as controlled substances are prohibited in jail.

"I didn't mean to appear aloof or cold, unfortunately that's just the way I come across, especially when I'm nervous…."

He said, "… in times of tragedy it's important not to lose yourself in grief and instead focus on whatever positives God has blessed you with. This is especially true when comforting a grieving loved one, like I was comforting my father in the first clip you'll hear, who in turn used what I said to comfort my heart-broken siblings.

"What I did was tragic. But it would be a lie to say that no good came out of it. What my lawyer consistently refused to mention at trial, despite my pleas, was the life-threatening danger my siblings were in. As her psychiatrist Dr. DeLeon stated, my mother was not a bad person, but she was a danger to herself and to others when not on her medication. And after she died, as my four siblings were brought back to my, father, his determination was proved true. All four boys were returned bruised and filthy (Ian could not know this first-hand, as he was in jail; Dejah says she has photographs that prove otherwise).

"And my brother with Down syndrome and brain damage had not been given his much-needed anti-brain seizure medication that entire time, for over a week, forcing him to undergo dozens of seizures a day. He was so unwell upon returning that he had to spend three days in the emergency room where he was diagnosed with advanced undernourishment and dehydration. Had he been in Chloe's and her co-conspirator's care for even a day longer, he would have died."

He claimed the police refused to act because a detective was a friend of the Millers and "lover of one of my mother's close friends. "

He also claimed that the Sheriff's Office gave some of his father's property collected in evidence "to the other family," until returned with a note of apology from the sheriff (it was a Eustis PD case, not the county's. Borders retired in 2017 and died in 2021.)

"Let me repeat. Had the children been in their care for a day longer, at least one of them in their care would have died. That is a fact. No person who actually cared about innocent victims would have wanted that. My dearly departed mother especially would not have wanted that."

Dejah, in an interview with me, said: "I have video and pictures of them the entire time they were in our care. We actually let them play outside, something they were no longer allowed to do usually. I have video showing them just minutes before they were picked up and pictures after they got all clean taking a bath.

"Tars was brought outside and with us when we took the kids out to each for what was the first time for most of them! Eric can tell you Tars lived in a playpen basically. We took him out.

"The inspector who was dating one of my mom's friends did nothing to help us in any way. Honestly, I was disappointed in how the entire case was handled. There was no special treatment." (She shared the photos with me, and they looked happy and well.. I'm not publishing the photos for privacy reasons.)

"I never said I was happy my mother died. Nor did I say I wasn't sorry. I was merely looking at the silver lining of a very dark cloud expressing thanks that the life of at least one innocent child I love was spared.

"There's a second clip. And regarding that clip, please believe me when I say I fully acknowledge that I killed my mother, though I still insist I was temporarily insane at the time. However, it must be understood that my mother died not once but twice. She died in the car by my hands but was resuscitated on the scene. This is why I was initially charged with attempted murder. She was not dead.

"When she was taken to the hospital in critical but stable condition, both she and the unborn baby were very much alive. Had she been left on life support, it is likely that she could have come to full term and delivered a happy, healthy baby. Sadly, I doubt she ever would have recovered from the injuries she received from my attack.

"But she wasn't left on life support. Not even for a week, Chloe, Cindy and others lied to the hospital claiming that my father was a person of interest in the case, though Sheriff Gary Borders has personally said my father was never a person of interest in the case (It was a Eustis Police case, not the county sheriff's office). And they got him barred from her room.

"While he was barred, they pulled the plug on her after only four days, killing her for the second and final time. That I killed her this second time is what I dispute in the clip you'll hear, because no one knows how long she could have lasted. She was critical but stable. It's possible that she could have survived for over a year and a day, at which point I wouldn't have been charged with murder, though I still would necessarily have to be charged for the crime I did commit. But she wasn't given a chance.

"I'm not disputing what I did, nor am I minimizing my crime in that clip. I am clarifying where my fault lies. Her death in the car was my fault and for that I am eternally sorry.

"Your honor, allow me to express my sorrow and remorse for the evil act I committed on March 13, 2019. I loved my mother unconditionally and it was the open secret that I was her favorite child. Please understand, though she was my stepmother, I never viewed her as that. I only called her my stepmother in my 911 call to be perfectly honest because I didn't want to get in any more trouble than I was already in.

"My biological mother was only my mother in a genetic sense. Sue-Ellen was my mother and I couldn't have loved her more, which makes what I did that much more tragic.

"Never had she and I been closer than during the last year of her life when I was training to be a professional wrestler and we finally had an interest in common. Never would I have hurt my mother under any circumstances, but especially after we became so close. Practically best friends. And especially not when she was carrying a child.

"The fact that I was unconscious of my actions at the time does nothing to ally my grief. I took two lives and I couldn't be sorrier.

"Please don't be afraid that I'm a threat to society. I am not, nor will I ever be. I am an extremely strait-laced homebody who had never done anything wrong before or since the horrible tragedy. I understand that I have to be punished, but please be lenient.

"I'm terribly sorry for the pain I caused and want the chance to prove that remorse by being a productive member of society. I am not a bad person, nor am I evil. Nor am I a threat to anyone or anything. I am a good boy who did a very bad thing after a week of abject misery and fear while suffering from unmedicated mental illness and under irreplaceable circumstances.

"None of that excuses what I did, but I pray you consider it. I want to be rehabilitated. I want to continue seeing my doctor. I want to continue taking all of my medication, most of which I can't so long as I'm locked up. Please help me get back in good standing with the world.

"One final thing. A large part of the DA's attack, the smoking gun if you will, was my use of the word 'argument' in my phone call with my father. Mr. Camuccio claimed that word showed I was angry, not afraid, moments before the attack. What nobody, not even my lawyer, felt it important to do was to define the word, to explain that argument in and of itself does not denote anger or hostility. It means, quote, a dispute where there is strong disagreement, end quote, or quote, a discussion in which reasons are advanced for or against for some proposition or proposal, end quote.

"That's why you hear phrases like a violent argument or a heated argument, because by itself argument is neither violent nor heated. Argument is an exchange of opposing ideas, which is exactly what my mother and I were engaged in in the car before I began to cry and blacked out.

"Had Mr. Hornsby presented this information at the time like I asked, perhaps the jury's verdict would have been different.

"I only bring this up to plead with you, your honor, to believe me when I say I never intended to harm my mother. I am not a threat to society. I am not a cold-blooded killer, nor do I have a homicidal temper. I had a psychotic break during a perfect storm of tragedy and I am terribly sorry for what I did. That's all I have to say. I'm very sorry. I never wanted any of this to happen. Thank you very much for your time and consideration. I have spoken."

Camuccio, seeking clarification on what Hornsby would be arguing from his motion of departure, asked about the fourth point in the memo.

"I'm not going to argue number four."

Ian spoke up: "Please argue number four."

"Okay. Well, never mind. I'll argue number four."

The fourth item on the lists stated: "The defendant requires specialized treatment for a mental disorder that is unrelated to substance abuse or addiction or for a physical disability, and the defendant is amenable to treatment."

Camuccio responded: "…there are multiple avenues and multiple resources for mentally ill people in the Department of Corrections. Obviously, they have a larger than proportional to society group of people that do suffer from various mental illnesses…."

BLAME GAME

Camuccio then presented two jail calls to the court that Ian made to his father after he was convicted.

"…I just saw Hornsby," Ian said.

"This early in the morning?"

"Yeah. It didn't go well. And I showed him my letter, but I'm not changing a word of it. But he's telling me, oh, you need to mention this, you need to not say that. I'm not doing what he says. And then it got heated. And then I asked him point blank, 'Do you believe my father did this? He said, 'I don't know what to believe. I slammed the phone on him. I said, 'I'll be seeing you in hell,' then walked out."

"Why did you do that?"

"Because he's not on our side. He doesn't care. All he wants to do is kowtow to them. He wants me to take [more] full responsibility than what I have. He wants to completely bury me for what happened."

"What did he say?"

"Like, if I can remember, I … apologized for being the major factor in her death at one point. He said, 'Major factor?'

"I said, 'Yeah. She wasn't dead. They pulled the plug on her. They killed her and the baby.'

"And he's trying to say that's not what happened. I said it is. He said, 'You killed Sue-Ellen.'

"I said, 'Fine but what about the baby?'

"I said she could have been [put into an] incubator. I said, 'I am admitting it was my fault. I'm not gonna take them all because to take the whole responsibility of that … do you think it's (indiscernible) an appeal, stuff like that? You can't appeal this because you already said this.'

"I'm not gonna take any more responsibility than what I actually directly did."

"Okay."

"Then he's saying I can't appeal because of my letters to you, and stuff like that, that I've never shown remorse because of the way I write, how I speak and stuff.

"At the beginning of my letter, my introductory letter, I have a page where I explain. I said I'm a little weird and a little bit about why, with the word twists that I used. It's because of what I read. It's how I am. It has nothing to do with disrespect. He wants me to get rid of that…."

He continued, saying: "There is a point in there where I say I'm sorry for what I did, because I am. I'm sorry I robbed you of the love of your life, and your last child. And I've robbed my siblings of a mother and another sibling. He wants me to get rid of mentioning you. Sorry, I'm not gonna do it. And he says, 'Well, but nobody's going to believe the (indiscernible) because nobody, nobody (indiscernible).' I said, 'That's your fault.' Not you, his."

"Don't do it."

"I'm unable to."

Ian, quoting Hornsby said, "You sound just like your father." Ian said he thanked him for saying that.

He went on to tell John that he wasn't going to lie, and Hornsby told him that he was "not in reality."

He continued, 'I killed her. They brought her back. She was never coming back alive, but she wasn't dead. I'm not the sole cause of her death. I'm just not gonna do it. Especially the baby."

John said he did not understand why Hornsby was talking about him.

"He tried to say you got me to kill her by the way you act and stuff. And he was trying to talk about how Chloe is so reliable."

Camuccio played another jail call recording from the next day, July 11.

Ian said: "I am upset because this has all happened and stuff. I'm not happy that I'm going to prison and stuff. But I guess the people... I don't (indiscernible) on this planet and four of them would die.... My life is gone but they are still alive."

Camuccio said the state was asking for a life sentence for the second-degree murder charge relating to Sue-Ellen, and 30 years for the death of the baby.

ESCAPE 'ORBIT'

Hornsby argued for a lighter sentence.

"Judge, I would point out to the court something that came out during trial and it's something that has struck me, is that, and so the court knows, obviously, Mr. Anselmo doesn't necessarily agree with the direction sometimes that I have taken with the case or the arguments that I have made. But ... "the overriding person in this entire case has obviously been his father, Miss Sue-Ellen's husband.

"And the one thing that has shown is that whenever someone has escaped his orbit, they have become a good person.

"We have Ms. Waite who escaped his orbit and I think we all agree is an extremely extraordinary person. You heard testimony, although you haven't heard from him, about their brother, Eric Anselmo, who escaped the obit and is doing very well.

"And then finally, unfortunately, this trial has been about the one person who escaped his obit but died tragically, and that's Sue-Ellen. But noticeably one of the first things, I believe it was what Ms. Miller said, is that within one week of escaping Mr. Anselmo, she showed various signs of this happy, positive person.

"Judge, obviously prison isn't an escape from Mr. Anselmo, but eventually over time with an appropriate prison sentence, I believe that he will be weaned off of [the] influence that is what caused us to be here today."

He continued, saying … "I ask the court to keep that in mind because we have seen through the trial that this very well could have been Rajko sitting next to me, if he had been 10 years older, based upon the video that we saw. Based upon the testimony of Ms. Waite, even what she said here today, it could have been Rajko. That's how powerful the influence was over these children."

He also cited the testimony of Cindy Miller, "that these children believe what they're saying because of the influence of the father."

Hornsby then made a surprising turn.

"Judge, it's undisputed that Mr. Anselmo had the capacity at the time that this incident with Mr. Anselmo occurred to appreciate the criminal nature of what he had done and to conform his conduct to the requirements of law, or that they were substantially impaired, which is another way of saying that he was suffering from diminished capacity at the time.

Diminished capacity is not a legal defense to a crime, but it is a mitigating circumstance.

"You heard from multiple mental health experts that all agreed that Mr. Anselmo suffers from a mental illness. They all agreed that he was off his medication through no fault of his own ...."

Even Dr. Werner agreed that he was going through withdrawal, though she had never heard of it being that severe, Hornsby said.

"When you combine that with the clear emotional, fragile state he was in, it's very clear that he lacked the ability to control himself and that he was unable to control his emotions or his conduct. And given that, judge, you should find that there's substantial evidence to support that departure ...."

He then argued that Ian needed specialized treatment for his mental illness.

"Judge, the third one is, you know, the defendant acted under extreme duress or under the domination of another. You know, my client cited a dictionary definition, and if you go to that, interestingly, domination is defined as more than just, you know, telling someone what to do. It can be someone's influence, preeminence over another, exercise of ruling power, governing or controlling influence on somebody...."

"It's so obvious that Mr. Anselmo, everybody testified that he was a dominating influence on everybody in this family."

He said Cindy Miller expressed it in her impact statement.

"Ms. Miller explained how that, because of Mr. Anselmo, she stopped having contact with her daughter. She also explained how that what Mr. Anselmo says, these children believe and follow. And even Ms. Waite said in her impact statement that these children, their memories, are suppressed and slowly erased because of, I don't know if you want to call it conditioning, or whatever you want to call it.

"Now, I'm not saying that Mr. Anselmo's father told him to go out and do this to Miss Sue-Ellen, but what I'm saying is that these children legitimately believed that Sue-Ellen was a danger to their other siblings, whether it's factually supported or not."

"... I don't think anybody disputes that he believes it to this day that his siblings were in mortal danger because of the influence of his father. And that his actions in going there, and as the testimony laid out, the purpose in going there was to try to, I guess, to bring the children back, or something of that nature. And that when she didn't, he snapped. I think that's the only logical conclusion to what happened is that he couldn't believe that someone was going against the father's control or desires.

"And I don't think that these children are liars, able to deal with people not obeying what their father wants.

'ARTLESS' STRANGLING

"Judge, the fourth one is, obviously, my most difficult argument to make, but I think it is supported by the evidence. The offense was committed in an unsophisticated manner. It was an isolated incident for which the defendant showed remorse.

"I understand that people listening may not think this was considered legally unsophisticated. But the case law that has interpreted similar acts, judge, has found that someone acting out in what we call a heat of passion in strangling someone, that is an artless, unsophisticated act. And that because of that, you could find that the act itself qualifies for the first prong.

"The second prong is obviously more difficult and depends on how you view Mr. Anselmo. Has he shown remorse? Judge, he explained to you why he said what he did. It's very clear that these children, and I think we got it, and I don't want to extrapolate from because I didn't ask her during the trial, and Ms. Waite said how Nico is still calling her, blaming her for Sue Ellen's death, and I'm almost 99 percent sure that what was discussed in the trial was that they blame her for the death because of what Mr. Anselmo said, is that they say because the family pulled the plug, they're actually the ones that caused Sue Ellen's death, as illogical as that may come across.

"But he's clearly shown that he is remorseful for what his acts were and what they did. And even, I think, what's a more accurate picture of who he was when you heard him on the 911 call when he called law enforcement and he was in tears.

"Finally, judge, number five grounds for departure. At the time of the offense the defendant was too young to appreciate the consequences of the offense. Judge, the case law has said that when you're making a determination of this statutory ground for departure, whether it's there, it's not the chronological age that matters, it's the evidence of emotional immaturity.

"Every single person that testified that either examined Mr. Anselmo or was a family member testified that he's a child in a man's body. All the experts, including Dr. Werner, said that he had, although he's biologically an adult, he's emotionally and mentally a child or child-like, I think was Dr. Werner's own statement.

He reminded the judge of Dejah's testimony about Ian playing with toys and how he liked being around the children. "You saw the pictures in the trial of how his room is still adorned with action figures in every single corner.

"And most importantly, judge, he lived an isolated life. He was completely isolated from the entire world, essentially. And his understanding of what he had done, I think, was clearly, given his immaturity, he didn't appreciate what he was doing or the seriousness of it because here is basically a child in a man's body thinking that he can solve the family's problems by bringing their mother back to their father.

"Judge, again, this is why we have judges to make these difficult decisions. I believe that there's an enormous amount of mitigating evidence within any portion of the record you listen to that would support any of the grounds for departure, and those would be upheld on appeal.

"I think the simplest one is obviously that Mr. Anselmo requires specialized treatment for mental disorder, he is amenable to treatment.

"The only question," he said, "is what's the appropriate sentence?"

He said talked to Cindy Miller and Dejah, and both said they wanted to see a long sentence. "…it's something I agree with to an extent," he said, but then he posed the question of just what that would look like. He referred to manslaughter cases with sentences of around 12 years.

"And here we have second-degree murder with an enormous amount of mitigating circumstances. And so, what is an appropriate sentence if you find a ground for departure? And obviously, once you find a ground for departure, the guideline doesn't matter. Judge, I think an appropriate long prison for Mr. Anselmo would be between 15 and 20 years.

"I think that's sufficient time for him to reflect on what happened. I think it's sufficient time for him to break the influence of his father. I think it's sufficient time for him to be rehabilitated."

Referring to Miller and Dejah, he said: "I don't want to put words in their mouths as I try to process what they're saying, but ...what they alluded to is that he has the potential to be a very productive person in this society. And 15 to 20 years from now puts him, you know, in his early 40s maybe, depending on how he's sentenced, to come to be apart from his influence, and be able to show that, like Dejah-Thoris, like Eric, like Sue-Ellen, that you break that orbit, you can be a good and productive person."

He said it would "sufficiently punish him for the actions he did under extreme and emotional distress, having gone through a childhood, that if you believe Ms. Waite, was one of the most traumatic childhoods that a child could be brought up in."

He said the sentence was appropriate under the circumstances, "and not trying to diminish the importance of either Sue-Ellen's life, or her unborn child's life."

Camuccio agreed with the law that allows a departure sentence if the defense meets its burden. Furthermore, he agreed that it met its burden on number two. "...the defendant requires specialized treatment for a mental disorder, unrelated to substance abuse or addiction, and the defendant is amenable to treatment...."

SHEER TORTURE

However, the state objected to departure on the other four points.

"…to give a departure in this case based on the mitigation outlined by Mr. Hornsby in this memorandum ignores the aggravation in this case and ignores the sheer torture, pain and suffering of Sue-Ellen when she was being strangled, not in one way, but in two different ways. Being struck in the face and having her jaw broken. Having her killed and the unborn child. We have two victims in this case.

"Focusing on Mr. Anselmo's mental health ignores all of that aggravation. But most importantly, the sheer volume of testimony and argument that Mr. Hornsby makes about the mitigation and about Mr. Anselmo's mental health condition that says his ability to conduct to the requirements of law was substantially impaired he says was undisputed.

"Well, that's just not true. Because the jury heard all of this evidence. They heard the testimony presented by the defense and all of these things, and all of his mental health conditions, and the fact that he didn't have his medications. And not only did they reject outright the defense of insanity, but they rejected the various lesser included offenses such as manslaughter. They found him guilty of second-degree murder, which means they found that at the time he strangled Sue-Ellen to death, killing her and her and her unborn child, he did so with evil ill will, hatred, spite. All of that rejects this memorandum and rejects the facts as proposed by the defense of what the evidence in this case was.

He said there was "absolutely no evidence whatsoever in this case that Mr. [John] Anselmo was the quote, dominant role in this case." He was not present when Ian "wrapped that cord around Sue-Ellen's neck, when he punched her in the face and broke her jaw, when he put his hands around her neck and strangled her until she died."

Camuccio also disputed the "unsophisticated" departure argument.

"The state is not alleging that the actions that happened in Sue-Ellen's vehicle was done so in a sophisticated manner," Camuccio said, but there are three "prongs," or hurdles that the defense must make in that argument.

"Mr. Anselmo does not have prior criminal history, so we're not saying that it was not isolated. However, the record is full of evidence showing that he showed absolutely no remorse whatsoever in this case.

"The fact that he continues to blame the family members who were forced to make the decision to withdraw life support to Sue-Ellen and tries to put a proportion of blame on them is quite offensive to the state. There were repeated time frames during the trial where the state was asking questions to the various law enforcement officers on the scene as to whether or not Mr. Anselmo ever asked how Sue-Ellen was doing. We asked questions about was he in a position to see the paramedics arrive and the things of that nature. And Mr. Hornsby made various arguments as to why I asked those questions.

"But those questions were really asked to show that Mr. Anselmo had absolutely no remorse for what he did. When he was at the hospital, when Sue-Ellen was also at the hospital receiving care for the injuries suffered by Ian Anselmo, he never once asked how is she doing, is she going to be okay?

He also noted that while Cindy Miller and Dejah-Thoris gave victim impact statements, "he sat there and did not react whatsoever. And then you heard those jail calls where he talks about how 'I'm not taking responsibility for stuff that other people did.' He says that 'what I did was a benefit to other people in the family.' That's not remorse. That's not remorse under any definition and they have not met their burden of establishing that prong.

"And then finally, at the time of the offense, the defendant was too young to appreciate the consequences of the offense."

He cited case law to bolster his argument and said, "Mr. Anselmo is a smart, eloquent man and there is absolutely no evidence whatsoever that is presented, despite his immaturity, that he did not appreciate the fact of the consequences of his actions and what will happen him based on this sentence.

"The state's position is the mitigation presented by the defense, most of which was categorically refused by the jury's verdict, does not and should not influence this court in its discretion to grant a downward departure due to the severely aggravated fact nature of this offense. He violently killed Sue-Ellen and thereby killed her unborn child, which he knew she was pregnant.

"The sheer amount of time that it would take in order to do this indicates and supports the jury's verdict of the depraved mind, the ill will, hatred, spite that was going through Mr. Anselmo at the time of this murder. And based on that, although there is legal grounds to support a departure if the court wished, the state is asking that grace not be extended to the defendant and he be given a life sentence."

Judge Welke recessed the court for 10 minutes. When he returned, he asked Hornsby "to present your client." Both stood.

"So, Mr., Anselmo, after having presided over the trial in this matter and having read the evaluations, the presentencing investigation, the motion for downward departure, the affidavit from the DOC, the letters in your support, and after hearing the victim impact statements, your statement, the jailhouse calls and the argument of counsel, the court finds that even if any of the mitigating factors apply, this court does not find any justification to apply them for a downward departure.

"Having been found guilty by a jury of your peers, I adjudicate you guilty, Mr. Anselmo, for the murder in the second degree of Sue-Ellen, I sentence you to life in prison with the Department of Corrections. And for the killing of Sue-Ellen's unborn child, I sentence you to 30 years Department of Corrections. The sentences will run concurrently."

CHAPTER 31

THE APPEAL

Anselmo was assigned an assistant public defender to file an appeal with the 5th District Court of Appeal, and that attorney stated: "Where the defendant established insanity by clear and convincing evidence and the state failed to rebut the defense, the trial court should have granted a motion for judgment of acquittal."[73]

"That's not true," Camuccio said. "I presented rebuttal."[74]

The appeal is still pending.

Requests for a motion of acquittal at the end of a trial are as routine as rain. The problem is, they are rarely granted.

A defense attorney must make the case that the state did not present enough evidence for a conviction. If the judge disagrees, he rules that there is enough to proceed and lets the jury decide. In insanity cases, a judge must also decide

---

73. Assistant Public Defender George D.E. Burden, Initial brief of appellant, Fifth District Court of Appeal, Case No. 5D224-2994, March 26, 2025.

74. Interview with Nick Camuccio, June 6, 2025.

if the defense presented "competent evidence" to prove insanity. By law, people are presumed sane.

Prosecutors don't have to present their own mental health experts. They could call witnesses or make their case through cross-examination. Camuccio, however, did call on Dr. Werner.

The attorney general's brief in support of conviction also cited evidence of Ian's state of mind.

Ian described himself as "level-headed" when texting Sue-Ellen hours before the attack. Body cam video recorded him as saying "I'm so sorry," and that his father would be angry with him.[75]

"This was strong proof that appellant *did know* what he was doing and *did know* that what he was doing was wrong," the brief stated.

The document also mentioned Dr. DeLeon's diagnoses. "… it was not until after the murder that Dr. DeLeon diagnosed appellant with PTSD, generalized anxiety disorder, and a personality of the schizotypal type. The doctor agreed that he relied on information from appellant and his family in making diagnoses and acknowledged that there was a chance the information was not accurate."

Dr. Buffington did not talk to Ian.

Dr. Saunders admitted that Ian could have been lying to him. He also conceded that because of his emotional state, "it was difficult to get a lot out of him."

---

75. Assistant Attorney General Deborah Chance, Answer brief of appellee, 5th District Court of Appeal, Case No. 5D224-2994, April 25, 2025.

He agreed that Ian made the 911 call, corrected an officer's spelling of his name, mentioned his rosary and remembered having an argument.

The brief mentioned among other things Dr. Werner's conclusion that Ian did not have PTSD prior to the homicide. It quoted the prosecutor's question: "No medical professional could come to the conclusion that the PTSD isn't a result of the violent act that he committed. Is that fair?"

Werner answered, "Yes, I believe so."

The brief also mentioned her conclusion that psychosis does not occur quickly or go away within a few minutes.

Then, of course, there was what Werner called "a lot of anger."

"He had previously threatened to disembowel her and choke her with her intestines...."

The defense brief claimed that Dr. Werner "was unable to disprove that he lacked the requisite state of mind for criminal liability."

It said that Ian was suffering from the withdrawal of his medications. "Moreover, the appellant hardly had any food or sleep due to the untreated depression and anxiety he suffered after his stepmother left the house with some of his younger siblings."

The document also said the fact that Ian talked to his toys right up to the murder "meant that he was susceptible to having a psychotic break."

The appellant public defender also cited Ian's claim and Buffington's opinion that the lack of memory about the murder was evidence of a psychotic break.

CHAPTER 32

WAS IT A CULT?

Was the Anselmo family a cult?

"I definitely think it's the toxic family system, without a doubt," said defense psychologist Dr. William Saunders. "And I think that his father did infect him quite a bit with a lot of ideas that weren't necessarily based on reality, that contributed to both trauma and ... his eventual psychotic break."

When Hornsby asked him to define "cult, he described it as "...typically a group of individuals that are ruled over by typically a single individual and similar in nature, the cult members are not allowed to reach out beyond cult members for support or for information. Their information is typically limited. There's a high degree of control the cult leader has over different members. And they're not allowed to have any kind of really independent thought, is the ultimate aim of most cults."

Hornsby planted the seeds early, during jury selection, when he asked an educator if a child could be "brainwashed." Then, he asked, "Is there anybody here who thinks brainwashing is voodoo, or fake or made up or stuff that defense attorneys like me kind of raise in cases?"

Finally, he asked, "… is anybody familiar with any cults, or some of you guys watch … true crime stuff. Anybody familiar with stuff like that? Can you have cult-like behavior in families?"

"Yes," one person answered.

The juror who answered yes to the true crime show question did not say which case it involved, but it could have been about the notorious teen vampire cult murders in Lake County, which made international headlines in 1996.

Sixteen-year-old cult leader Rod Ferrell came to Eustis from his home in Kentucky in November of that year with three followers. His goal was to gather up two his former classmates at Eustis High School and run away to New Orleans to start a vampire "family."

After meeting with his 15-year-old friend Heather Wendorf at Greenwood Cemetery (yes, that cemetery) and becoming her vampire "sire" in a blood-drinking "crossover" ritual, he beat her parents to death with a crowbar and stole their SUV. The group, including Heather, were captured three days later. She was not charged in a decision that is controversial to this day.

A defense attorney exclaimed, "This is not a Charles Manson case."[76]

True. Manson's cult "family" murdered pregnant actress Sharon Tate and several others in 1969. He remains the granddaddy of all nightmares, but there were some similarities.

---

76. Frank Stanfield, *Cold Blooded, A True Crime Story of a Murderous Teenage Vampire Cult,* WildBlue Press, 2021.

Manson isolated his followers at remote desert ranches and preached delusional beliefs until his followers were completely sold.

Heather told investigators that Ferrell was isolating her from her parents. "...he wanted to break the ties, we wanted to break the ties to Florida."

FBI profiler John Douglas said of Manson: "He used sleep deprivation, sex, food control and drugs to gain complete dominance, like a prisoner-of-war situation. Everything was black and white and only Charlie knew the truth."[77]

Dejah testified that John isolated the family, including with physical, emotional and sexual abuse, food control, and sleep deprivation. Hornsby noted that Ian had been medicated for years.

Author Sean Dolan wrote: "The more a person has invested in a cult – in terms of such things as time, money and emotions – the more unlikely it is that he or she will be able to do what it takes to leave. By that point, the typical cult member will have surrendered so much of his or her previous life – friends, family, romantic relationships, education, work and career money, years of a life -- that it becomes more difficult to admit to having been manipulated or tricked."[78]

Hornsby marveled at Dejah's ability to leave. It took Dejah's sexual assault allegation for Sue-Ellen to walk away.

"Abusive families are like cults," said Dr. Glenn Doyle on his website.[79]

---

77. *Mind Hunter*

78. Sean Dolan, *Everything You Need to Know about Cults*, New York, The Rosen Publishing Group, Inc., 2000.

79. http://useyourdamnskills.com/2024/01/18/abusive-families-are-like-cults/

"Abusive families ... often require members to adhere to a code of silence— especially to anyone outside the group," he said.

Dejah's testimony about the "Anselmo Code" says it all.

It is difficult to "opt out," members feel pressured to say everything is fine. Rajko and Nico testified that things were good. Dejah and Eric say they were coached.

"Like cults, abusive families often limit the opportunities for members to socialize or interact with people not in the group— and, like cults, abusive families often frame this as being for members' "own good."

"We were not to speak unless spoken to," Dejah said.

Outsiders are denigrated. John said the neighborhood children "suck."

Abusive families, like cults, cultivate the belief that loyalty to the group is the top priority in members' lives— and if members have a problem with that, it demonstrates a problem with their "character." John accused Dejah of being a liar, mentally ill, and a pathetic person seeking attention.

Embark Behavioral Health, which operates mental health treatment centers for preteens, teens, and young adults, offers its own perspective on cults, including the idea of the "golden child."

"The golden child, hero, or saint is the favored child who receives special treatment, praise, and high expectations or an only child who can do no wrong," said Jenilyn Bartolo, a counselor with Embark. "The focus on the golden child often masks a family's underlying issues. If there are siblings, parents will say to the other kids, 'Why can't you behave more like this child?' But the golden child also has a lot of expectations put on them and can be a very lonely kid."[80]

She said there is also a scapegoat or black sheep, "the family member who's blamed for the home's problems and difficulties. In some cases, this role serves as a distraction from the family's real problems."

"There was always a whipping boy," Eric said in an interview with me, and he played that role. Ian used to be the golden boy, Eric said, then it was Rajko. That angered Ian and made him even more willing to do anything he could to please John, he said.[81]

That included trying to get Sue-Ellen to return the children, which he did, either by texting "I love you," or claiming that she was not a mother to him.

The jurors said they felt sorry for Ian at times and were struck by his reaction at the crime scene: "My father is going to be so mad."

"I feel like he [John] stirred the flames. Ian took the heat," Eric said. "I think he would have done it anyway."

Bartolo also talked about "parentified children." In a healthy family, the parents provide emotional security and meet the children's needs.

John describes himself as the maternal figure, but the children pointed to Ian as a crucial caregiver.

"The peacemaker or mediator tries to resolve conflicts and maintain harmony within the family, often at their own expense. They may sacrifice their own emotional needs to

---

80. https://embarkbh.com/tratment/therapies/family-therapy/ dysfunctional-familyroles/
81. Interview with Eric Anselmo, June 17, 2025.

provide what they perceive their siblings or parents need. Parents often create these roles in their children when one of them makes negative or harsh statements about the other parent."

This burden clearly fell on Dejah. She testified that she was so close to Ian that she sometimes shielded him from blame and the wrath of John.

There are also insufficient boundaries and a lack of healthy conflict resolution, with children more prone to arguing with each other.

"Ian threatened to kill me many times," Eric said.

It's a far different picture than the one John depicted in his deposition: "He's the sweetest, kindest, kid you'll ever meet, you'll ever meet, you know."

Doyle writes on his webpage: "When we've grown up in an abusive family, and/or been part of a cult, we can't pretend that's NOT a part of our history. We need to do what we need to do to recover. No shame. It wasn't your fault. It wasn't your choice. But recovery, is."

Was it a cult? "It was 100 percent a cult," Eric said.

CHAPTER 33

THE PROBLEM WIH MENTAL HEALTH EXPERTS

It is virtually impossible today to watch a crime show without seeing dazzling displays of DNA developments, phone and computer records, surveillance videos, medical examiner discoveries and other scientific wizardry that have changed court cases forever.

There is still, however, what Hornsby called the "soft science" of psychology and psychiatry. Of course, he didn't say that until he was cross-examining the state's expert, Dr. Tonia Werner.

The reason defense attorneys ask if an expert has ever testified for the state is to detect "bias," he said.[82]

He had Werner describe her work, including drafting reports and doing other work on cases where she was not called to testify. That can happen for a lot of reasons. An expert might help a legal team prepare for a trial, gain insight into the defendant, maybe even act as a jury consultant. Then, of course, the expert's opinion might not fit the defense team's

---

82. Werner trial testimony, Vol. VIII, April 11, 2024.

strategy, possibly even coming to the opposite conclusion. It's standard practice. Ethics prohibit the other side from hiring the expert once he leaves the first team.

The experts are to give their opinions within psychological "certainty." Yet, two experts could have vastly different opinions based on their interpretation of tests, analysis of family history and understanding of the case.

But sometimes questions are raised about the experts' motives, methodology, and head-scratching approaches to head-shrinking.

Werner was asked in her deposition if she had any "concerns with Dr. DeLeon's, I guess, treatment? Is there a conflict?"[83]

"I think there's a conflict in that he had both of them under his care, yes. And I think he understood that which is why he sat down on his own and wrote these huge, long reports after the fact that one of his patients killed another one of his patients. Kind of a cover-your-fanny type thing."

"Is that the first thing you thought when you read that report?"

"Yes, ma'am, absolutely."

"Okay. So, you think he came up with this PTSD to kind of cover his butt?"

"I don't know why he came up with it at this point, but I think that's why he wrote those two long reports on the two of them. Nobody asked – he acknowledged nobody asked him to do that. He did that on his own accord. And if I remember correctly, they were very lengthy."

---

83. Werner deposition, March 3, 2023.

"And the PTSD in terms of the stressors, if Dr. DeLeon was treating both Sue Ellen and Ian, he's not going to necessarily acknowledge that Ian is being victimized….," she said.

"You would be a mandatory reporter. It's his job and his legal responsibility to mandatorily report any abuse that's going on to a child under his care."

"Is it possible that he failed being a reporter?"

"He may have. Or he didn't feel it rose to that level, I don't know."

Camuccio did not touch on that issue, but he was quick to point out in trial cross-examination of DeLeon that his final report included all kinds of new diagnoses.

DeLeon, in a phone interview with me, said he wrote two reports "to make it more concise."[84]

He denied ever being told about any alleged child abuse.

At first, DeLeon was reluctant to talk to me and asked if I had Ian's consent. I told him that I received DeLeon's second report from Ian himself.

I wrote to Ian on June 3, 2025. "I feel it is only fair to give you a chance to tell your side of the story, especially since you did not testify."

He turned me down, which was not a surprise.

"From the beginning, you have treated me and my family unfairly. It is clear that you are biased and prejudiced and care more about making a name for yourself than about the truth."

---

84. DeLeon interview, July 26, 2025.

That wasn't a surprise either. His father dislikes me intensely, I believe, because he had no control over what I wrote for the *Daily Commercial*.

DeLeon's report on Sue-Ellen, dated May 20, 2020, was written in an objective-sounding, psychiatric style, but he described her history in a hard, unblinking manner.

It said, for example, that she blamed her parents for self-destructive, relationship-ending, rebellious behaviors.

The report quoted John saying he was not aware of these behaviors when they married, but he put a stop to them. "I asked directly if she ever was abused in any way by him," DeLeon wrote. "She said her husband was very loving and not abusive."

He quoted her remarks in a letter to the children in 2015: "I love your daddy. I feel like the luckiest girl to have him. I look back at the beginning of our relationship and see every last thing he has done for me over the years. No matter what a piece of shit I was."

He then quoted her from a letter he said was addressed to him: "I know Johnny is looking out for my best interest. I have asked him to guide me so I can get the best possible treatment."

DeLeon wrote: "Sue-Ellen refrained from providing to me the details of the extent of her mood swings and other symptoms in fear that I would add medications that could make her gain weight, or worse yet, send her to a psychiatric hospital."

He said, "little by little some information leaked out during conversations with her, her husband and her children."

He also reported: "She told me a couple of times that she would have strange experiences of feeling, seeing, or hearing things that weren't there. The family said these were more frequent but refused to elaborate in fear of her hospitalization.

He continued: "She had good periods of stability while treated with medications."

HeHH wasn't totally unsympathetic. "My feeling always was that, for her, the priority was always for the physical and mental well-being of the others in her family. This, however, was drastically in contrast to the opinion of her family, who believed that at home everything was about herself, and that she was trying to depict a much more positive image to me."

He diagnosed her with bipolar disorder, borderline personality disorder and ADHD. He prescribed Lexapro and Vyvanse.

"The establishment of these diagnoses was a very gradual process that took years and a substantial amount of collateral information."

Did he have all the information he needed?

At trial, Camuccio asked: "Now, in your practice, the vast majority of the information that you have to rely on in making these diagnoses comes from your patients, is that fair?"[85]

"Yes."

"All right. And you are obviously aware that he is facing charges for murder?"

"Yes."

---

85. DeLeon trial testimony, Vol. VI, April 10, 2024.

"And so, you would agree with me that in accepting self-reports from someone in that situation, you have to be kind of leery about what they're telling you about that?"

"Well, there's always a chance that, that the information is not accurate, but I do tend to trust what they are saying."

"Okay, so you trust what these people are saying about the events that led to Sue-Ellen's murder?"

"That's the nature of the patient/doctor relationship."

I asked DeLeon if patients typically lie to therapists and themselves initially.

"No, that's not true," he said.

"And doesn't the public think of therapists as human lie detectors, able to discern the truth?"

"That's not fair to say," he said.

DeLeon today acknowledges that "they withheld a lot of information from me." He said he if had known about Sue-Ellen's alleged suicide attempts, for example, "I would have definitely had her Baker Acted, (involuntarily committed to a psychiatric hospital)."

DeLeon said it was not unethical for him to treat more than one person in a family. "There is not a rule on that." It happens when there are limited resources for patients in the area. For him, it began when he was treating the children.

He said he has learned a lot since the Anselmo case.

"They don't come to me anymore," he said of the family.

Hornsby asked DeLeon about John and Sue-Ellen's efforts to get a refill of Ian's prescription. He then asked, "… are you up there lying for Mr. Anselmo to cover your butt?"

"Absolutely not."

"So, Mr. Camuccio is suggesting that …. Obviously collateral information is important, right?"

Hornsby also asked: "I agree 100 percent, John Anselmo probably isn't the most honest broker to rely on by himself, right?"

"I cannot make that judgment call."

What did he mean by that? That he could not tell if John was giving him straight answer after years of treating the family?

DeLeon told me that he relied on his own records in writing the 2020 report, so he did not read the Eustis Police report where Sue-Ellen described John as "very controlling" and verbally abusive, nor did he talk to her divorce attorney about her fear of violent retribution.

He did not talk to Dejah at that time, who mentioned the Anselmo or "Family" code," or to Eric after he left home. Eric said in his 2025 interview with me that the children had been "coached" and that they grew up thinking violent punishment was normal.

What about the unfortunate well-known trend of domestic violence victims blaming themselves? "You are not crazy and you don't deserve to be told you are because you get mad or fight back when you are provoked in such terrible ways," Dejah wrote in her letter to Sue-Ellen.

It is unclear if DeLeon read Dejah's letter.

He discounted Dejah's allegation of sexual abuse in his 2020 report, calling it "false." The police report, however, said there was "insufficient evidence" to prosecute or make an arrest. That's a big difference, and it was not surprising considering the passage of time, no collaborative witness, and no physical evidence. In other words, it was an unfortunate, common problem for prosecutors: Her word against his.

He apparently did not read the text messages between John and Sue-Ellen. Did he read the letters Ian wrote from jail, letters that were published in the newspaper in 2019?

Did he read John's deposition, where, for example, Ian reportedly begged him to have Sue-Ellen involuntarily committed to a psychiatric hospital but he refused because she might lose her customers? This happened when she allegedly put a gun to her head, overdosed, and cut herself.

Was that an example of John looking out for her "best interest?"

Dejah made a scathing accusation about DeLeon in her victim impact statement.

"Nico is sending emails out to anyone she can with my mother's mental health records from Dr. DeLeon."

She said in an interview with me that the week that Sue-Ellen left she urgently scheduled a meeting with Dr. DeLeon to tell him that she had been coached to [not] reveal the truth behind her so-called mental health problems. Dr. DeLeon knew of this urgent phone call, but not the point of the meeting.

"And when I came myself to tell him after my mother was murdered, he would not swallow his pride and admit a patient of his had been coached."[86]

DeLeon denied "brushing off" Dejah.

Dejah recalled the conversation she had with her mother about the attempted emergency appointment. "She said it

---

86. Interview with Dejah, July 8, 2025.

would just have to wait a couple of days to tell him the truth and then she would feel so much better. But she was killed before the appointment. We also heard Johnny telling her what to say at the appointments all those years."

THE OTHER EXPERTS

Dr. Saunders told Camuccio that he reviewed records, text messages and bodycam videos, but made no reference to what Ian said about the murder.

"And that's because you didn't ask him about what happened that day; you relied on all these other sources, correct?[87]

Saunders said he tried but Ian was too "distraught."

Buffington did not interview Ian.

COURTROOM STRATEGY

Prosecutors and defense attorneys have a long history of duking it out over mental health expert testimony.

In 1995, Lake County residents were shocked by what was then a rare occurrence in America: a school shooting.

Keith Johnson, 14, pulled out a gun and fired 13 shots at his 13-year-old verbal tormentor, sending middle-school students and teachers scurrying for cover, and leaving Joey Summerall dead in a pool of blood on the sidewalk.

At his trial the following year, a defense expert testified that Johnson was suffering from "battered child syndrome."[88]

---

87. Saunders trial testimony, Vol. VIII, April 11, 2024.
88. Frank Stanfield, *Vampires, Gators and Wackos*, WildBlue Press, 2022.

But the prosecutor pointed out that there was no such syndrome listed in the *Diagnostic Statistical Manual of Mental Disorders*, the "bible" for the American Psychiatric Association. It was a takeoff of the battered spouse syndrome, where fear for one's life results in justifiable self-defense.

Johnson was found guilty of murder and sentenced to life in prison.

Two years later, the elected state attorney himself took the lead in prosecuting Rod Ferrell Like the Keith Johnson case, the prosecutors did not bring in their own expert, choosing instead to defuse the defense experts' testimony on cross-examination.

Ferrell wasn't claiming insanity, but because it was a death penalty case, his attorneys were allowed to present mitigation experts, who diagnosed him with various disorders, including schizotypal.

His lawyers also claimed that he had suffered multiple head traumas and childhood encephalitis, but as it turned out, there were no medical records to prove it.

The prosecutor in his opening argument told jurors to treat the experts like every other witness. "Listen to what they have the ability to know, those facts. And listen to how they used those facts in arriving at a conclusion. Because they are like everybody else. They come to you with some presumption of expertise but listen to what they had to work with and how they worked with it. And I think you will see that it is true, if you put garbage in you can't help but get garbage out."[89]

The defense attorney objected but the judge allowed it. "That's a fair comment," he said.

---

89. Frank Stanfield, *Cold Blooded, A True Crime Story of a Murderous Teenage Vampire Cult*, WildBlue Press, 2021.

The state attorney attacked the tests that the expert performed, pointing out that there was no safeguard against malingering, "purposely and consciously faking illness for some sort of gain, be it to get away from a crime you are being charged for, to try to get money in some way, things like that."

He also pounced on the diagnoses, pointing out that under the DSM, it could be classified as common anti-social behavior, typical of juvenile delinquency and lying,

Ferrell accused his grandfather of rape, which he denied.

The psychiatrist said he did not do any testing of Ferrell's mother, yet child neglect and family dysfunction was a huge part of the defense.

Like with Ferrell, no medical records were presented in Ian's trial to prove John's claim about him being born with the umbilical cord wrapped around his neck.

One expert said Ferrell's family was the most dysfunctional he had ever seen. And while there are many, many dissimilarities between the two cases, psychologists could have almost been talking about Ian.

Like Ferrell, Ian was sentenced to life without the possibility of parole.

CHAPTER 34

BLAMING THE VICTIM

Is there anything more disgusting than blaming the victim? Especially when she is not alive to defend herself? Yet, that is what John did to try and save Ian from a life behind bars and to try and preserve his own credibility. Sue-Ellen was clearly a victim, and not just a murder victim.

In her "Dear Mommy" letter, Dejah wrote: "Every time I saw you get hit it was like I was getting hit myself. Every time you cried my heart hurt for you and it was so terrible hearing you beg for help and for me to be so helpless and not be able to do anything."

It is important to note that Sue-Ellen never said, "Oh, that didn't happen." Nor did she doubt what Dejah said about being sexually abused. "It was so hard on me, being pressured in every way to try and replace you 'cause you guys were having issues."

How painful it must have been when Dejah added: "I don't fault you at all for any of the issues you guys had, just so you know."

One could be an armchair quarterback and say, "Well, Sue-Ellen should have left him a long time ago," but people stay married for a lot of reasons, including concerns about children, retaliation, and financial fears. Religious beliefs can also play a role. The two argued about Catholic annulment versus divorce. John told her that she would be committing adultery if she divorced him and married someone else.

"…I am allowed to divorce, just not allowed to remarry. I'm fine with that. I have no desire to be in a relationship," she said in a text.

Then, there is love, the overpowering emotion that defies rational explanation, especially when a lover switches from kisses to beatings.

Domestic violence victims often wrongly blame themselves.

This is not a new phenomenon. People today use the term "gaslighting" loosely to describe lying. The term actually comes from the 1944 movie *Gaslight* with Ingrid Bergman and Charles Boyer. In the film, the manipulative husband tries to convince his wife that she is losing her mind.

The Anselmo version shows up in heated text messages. "Please put into perspective that you are with child and off your meds."

In another he says, "I still have your notebooks about going crazy and your letters to the kids. Please just talk to me."

John claimed Sue-Ellen struck him. The children said she rebuffed him romantically.

"I don't blame her," Eric Anselmo says today.[90]

Eric left the household on March 6, 2021, two years to the day after Sue-Ellen left with her biological children, so he

---

90. Interview with Eric Anselmo, June 17, 2025.

is free from what Hornsby called "conditioning like a dog." Eric said John also coached the children on what to say to the authorities.

Dejah testified that she was conditioned to only remember the good things.

John's allegations of Sue-Ellen throwing plates, lashing out and banging head against wall were true, Eric said. "She felt like there was no control. She was at a loss about what to do."

As for the cheating allegation he said, "I wouldn't blame her if she did."

He said he will never forget the day Ian ran to him in the garage where he was sleeping to prevent John from killing her after he accused her of having an affair. "He had his knees on her chest and was beating her."

"I look at my wife now and I just can't imagine doing it to her," Eric said. "My response would be, 'Go find someone better.'"

John denied hitting Sue-Ellen in his deposition. "My heart is broken that she lied and said I hit her. I am broken, but I still love her. And she's still the mother of my children. But now I got to try to save my son. I don't want you to take him away. He's just a little boy. What he did was wrong and so F'ed up, but he didn't mean to."

John didn't seem to have any credibility with jurors, however.

"The easiest way to explain it was that he was very arrogant, a big line of B.S. You couldn't get past that arrogance," said juror Danny Wright.[91]

---

91. Interview with jurors, June 6, 2025.

"The kids were victims," said juror Desiree Cohrn. "The father used them to get what he wanted."

Sue-Ellen's friends and coworkers described John as "very controlling," but they did not want to be identified by name in news stories for fear of retribution.

It was not an irrational fear. A former teacher coworker of John's said she was accosted in a store, and that John went to her husband's place of work with the intention of fighting him. He also reportedly wanted to fight two young men at a vocational school when he misinterpreted a casual nod in Dejah's direction.

Coworkers said he made Sue-Ellen wear long, conservative dresses and drove her to work. Dejah said he routinely went through her text and phone messages. John admitted that he forbade her from cutting men's hair after she allegedly cheated on him. That led to an almost deadly confrontation with a man who tried to make an appointment. The man fired a rifle round into the ground when John and Ian approached his home.

How controlling is it when you pit children against your wife?

The day Sue-Ellen left and went with Dejah to the Eustis Police Department she said John had "brainwashed" the children into thinking she was the "bad guy."

When Nico was asked about Sue-Ellen's role in the household, she replied: "Sue-Ellen is not a role, just an entity. She caused problems, she was disruptive."

Dejah wrote in her letter: "You're my mother and I never turned my back on you no matter how many times my dad tried to get me to while everyone else tried to rat you out and get brownie points for 'telling on you.' I'd rather get conceited remarks from my dad than see you get hurt by his words or hands."

Sue-Ellen told police she figured the reason Dejah left home was "to get away from John because he is verbally abusive and very controlling."

She was afraid for her own safety by that time.

"The Domestic Violence Service Network reports that 'The time surrounding leaving their abuser is the most dangerous time for a victim. Risk of lethality is severely increased if the abuser feels they are losing control over the victim. As reported by the United States Department of Justice, 75 percent of homicide victims and 85 percent of women who experienced severe but non-fatal domestic violence had left or tried to leave their abuser within the past year."[92]

Every aspect of the children's lives was controlled, from what they were allowed to watch on TV, to virtual home schooling, prohibiting them from having friends, driving, or having phones. Some of the rules were bizarre. "I never wanted to scandalize my daughters and for them to see a boy's private part so the boys changed the boys' diapers.

The rules were enforced with frequent and abusive punishment.

"I lived it," Eric said. A better way of phrasing it was that he survived it.

"...he got beatings to the point where my dad would tell us that we needed to get Eric away from him or he was going to kill him," Dejah said.

---

92. Patricia Fersch, "Does It Really 'End With Us'? Why The End Of An Abusive Relationship Is The Most Dangerous Time For The Survivor," Forbes, Jan. 7, 2025.

The kids were made to sleep outdoors or on the floor of the garage, Dejah was made to do pushups until she collapsed, and Eric was deprived of food for up to 36 hours.

The campaign to besmirch Sue-Ellen's character continued after her death. One day during the trial, John showed up with a thick loose-leaf binder with evidence, he said, of Sue-Ellen's mental illness. I explained that I was not planning on writing a book on the case, so I passed. I later changed my mind. Besides, I told him, I was going to include his testimony in my trial coverage for the *Daily Commercial*. His accusations are included in this book. Some of the unflattering material was included in the package I received from Ian.

Dejah said Nico continued sending out blistering accusations online, including calling her a "manipulative parasite."

Dejah said John had a message for her after her mother was hospitalized: "I should kill myself."

Perhaps the most hurtful act of all occurred when John had Sue-Ellen's body exhumed.

"I'm just hurt that he's going to this length so spite me," Dejah said at the time. "He should let us grieve in our own way."

"She was a magnificent human being, very loving, caring, compassionate," Eric said of Sue-Ellen. "My last words to her were, 'I hate you.' I wish I could take that back."

EPILOGUE

Richard Hornsby was right when he told jurors that they would feel sorry for everyone in the family, even Ian somewhat. Everyone, that is, with the exception of John Anselmo.

Of course, jury instructions instruct the members not to use sympathy in their deliberations, probably the most difficult order, and the one most tempting to disobey.

The allegations against John are shocking: psychological domination warfare, domestic violence, sexual assault, blaming the victim, and creating a family cult sealed with a code of silence.

It is a testament to the human spirit that Dejah and Eric escaped to begin a lifetime of healing and the kind of love they deserve.

One has to wonder how the rest of the children will fare. Ian will have to try to get his head straight in prison, not exactly a place best known for rehabilitation. Cindy Miller said she would be praying for him, so anything is possible.

His case is on appeal. Anything is possible there. The courts, especially the U.S. Supreme Court, keeps moving the goal post, with the death penalty and youthful offenders being the most recent examples. Neither is applicable in this case.

For now, at least, the system worked. A jury of his peers concluded that he did not meet the criteria of temporary insanity.

The case did not cast mental health experts in a favorable light. Hopefully, someday mental health professionals, legislators and regulators will make some changes. Camuccio's charge that one expert disregarded facts because it didn't fit his narrative is just one example.

The tragic death of Sue-Ellen also laid bare the horror of domestic violence.

Over the years, I have covered so many cases that ended in death, from a young German immigrant who was killed and stuffed into a refrigerator, to a highly respected hospital administrator who was murdered by her husband at their home in an exclusive private airport community.

Those who operate shelters advise victims to make a plan, save some money, pack a go-bag and be aware that they face the greatest danger when they leave.

Too many women, they say, believe their lover when they promise never to hit them again.

Miller pointed out in her victim impact statement that Sue-Ellen's story has provided information and hope to victims, including one woman who was in fear for her life from an abusive stepson.

Most comforting of all was Miller's statement bolstered by her faith: "There are no tears in heaven."

R.I.P. Sue-Ellen.

For More News About Frank Stanfield,
Signup For Our Newsletter:

http://wbp.bz/newsletter

Word-of-mouth is critical to an author's long-
term success. If you appreciated this book please
leave a review on the Amazon sales page:

https://wbp.bz/graveyardmurderr

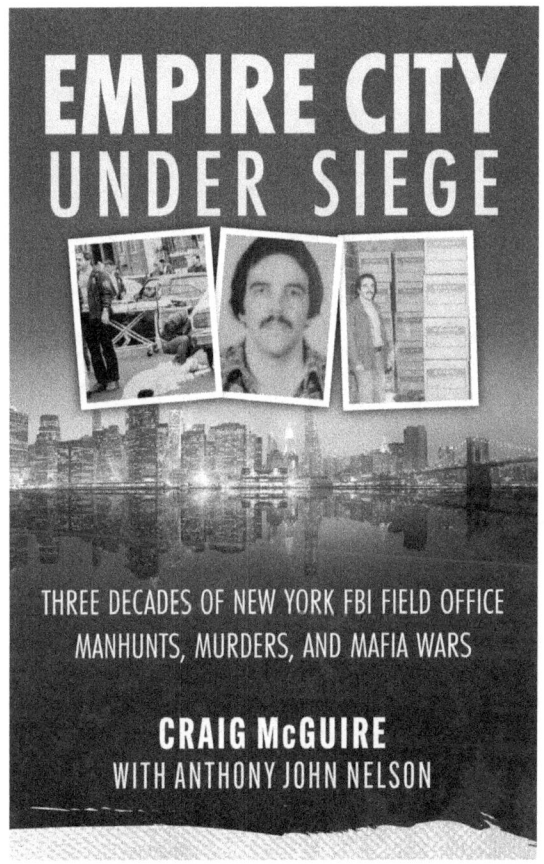

EMPIRE CITY UNDER SIEGE

https://wbp.bz/empirecity

www.ingramcontent.com/pod-product-compliance
Lightning Source LLC
Chambersburg PA
CBHW061604120626
46550CB00004B/1608